PROBLEMS IN CIVILIZATION

David H. Pinkney,
General Editor

PROBLEMS IN CIVILIZATION

THE ORIGINS
OF A
TRAGEDY

July 1914

Edited with
an Introduction by

Samuel R. Williamson, Jr.

The University of North Carolina
at Chapel Hill

The Forum Press, Inc.
Arlington Heights, Illinois 60004

84 85 86 87 88 CM 10 9 8 7 6 5 4 3 2

Printed in the United States of America.

Library of Congress Catalog Card Number: 80-657-43

ISBN: 0-88273-409-1

Theobald von Bethmann Hollweg
German Chancellor, 1909-1917

CONTENTS

INTRODUCTION

JUNE 28, 1914. Two shots were fired at a street corner in the Bosnian capital of Sarajevo in the Austro-Hungarian monarchy. Within minutes the heir to the monarchy, the Archduke Franz Ferdinand, and his wife Sophie were dead. Within six weeks Europe was at war. Four and one-half years later the royal couple had been joined in death by at least 8,538,315 combatants and 12,618,000 civilians. This unprecedented human carnage was matched by the material and economic damage: at least $36,760,000,000 in property destroyed. When the fighting finally ended in November 1918, four empires no longer existed: the German, the Austro-Hungarian, the Russian, and the Ottoman. In Russia, moreover, not the long-feared socialists, but the Bolsheviks—feared even more—were in power.

For over sixty years historians, politicians, journalists, and the public have asked the question: Why did the shots at Sarajevo set in motion the events that led to World War I? Why did the war come then and not in one of the earlier crises? What did the statesmen think they could achieve by force that could not be gained by negotiation? Who was "guilty" of such "stupidity"? Or who had plotted this affair? What had blinded nearly all to the dangers that might come from a war, not the least of which was the very destruction of the governments, societies, and ways of life that they were fighting to defend? Because World War I is one of history's seminal events, it must be—like the American Civil War, the French Revolution or the Reformation—studied, restudied, and contemplated by each generation of scholars and students. No understanding of the developments of the twentieth century is possible without an appreciation of the significance of the outbreak of war in 1914 and of the subsequent impact of that war upon first European and then world history.

But there are other, more specific reasons for examining why war came in the summer of 1914. First, the political life of Europe in the 1920s and 1930s cannot be understood without considering the debate over who started the war; second, the issue influenced the character of much of German intellectual and academic life during the 1960s when the question of Germany's role in 1914 was abruptly reopened; and finally, the similarities between the world of alliances and arms races in the years before 1914 and the international situation of the early 1980s pose crucial questions about the future of modern civilization.

Wartime accounts about who started the fighting were followed in 1919 by the declaration of the victorious powers that Germany and Austria-Hungary had planned and willed the war. Those two powers were charged with war guilt for starting the conflict and held responsible (through reparation payments) for restoring some of the material and human destruction the war had caused. Almost immediately this verdict was challenged, in Germany, of course, but also in France, Britain, and the United States. Many liberals thought the accusations one-sided and unfair; others thought they failed to deal with the complexities of international politics. The German government, not surprisingly, launched a major effort to "revise" the verdict of the Versailles Treaty. One German soldier-turned politician and political agitator, Adolf Hitler, soon became the most famous revisionist of all. His tirades about war guilt, coupled with other attacks upon the victorious powers and the new German government, provided a rallying cry for many discontented Germans. Hitler's accession to power in 1933 owed much to his manipulation of the war guilt issue. Further, when his own hegemonic aims began to become a reality in the late 1930s, memories of 1914—and the carnage that followed—exercised a deep influence upon French and British statesmen as they sought to appease the dictator. Moreover, the interwar debate over the outbreak of war in 1914 convinced many Americans that a policy of isolation and aloofness from European affairs was in the national interest. Thus Washington also responded late to the strategic threat posed by Hitler.

The second impact of the debate over July 1914 came in the decade of the sixties, the result of a prominent German historian's declaring to his fellow countrymen that yes, they were responsible for World War I. This assertion by Fritz Fischer in his 1961 study, *Griff nach der Weltmacht (Germany's Aims in the First World War)* shocked many in West Germany: historians, veterans of both wars, and the German political community. Bitter debates followed among German academics, at first along age and ideological lines, then later on more conventional historical issues about the use of evidence, the lack of comparative perspectives, and historical determinism. Nor was the West German government entirely aloof, at one point attempting to hamper Fischer's travels abroad and making evident its displeasure at his reopening an issue long considered, if not taboo, at least closed. The Fischer controversy thus came to dominate the development of German historical studies in the 1960s.

Finally, there are certain uncomfortable parallels between the diplomatic and political world of pre-1914 Europe and that of the early 1980s. In 1914 the Triple Entente competed with the Triple Alliance; today NATO is challenged by the Warsaw Pact. No historian thinks in terms of historical repetition and most would caution against drawing historical lessons. Yet one can view the existence of competing alliance structures and recurrent arms races as comparable phenomena, while the problem of expansionist tendencies and conscious status quo efforts to retain dominance have parallel aspects. Some observers would see in present-day Yugoslavia and other East European countries much of the fragility that was present in 1914. Thus an understanding of why war came in 1914 may alert the student, the scholar, and even the citizen to some of the dimensions of the problem of peace and war—dimensions not only essen-

tial to historical study, but possibly to humankind's survival.

I

The historical and political debate about July 1914 has had four generally distinct phases: that of the wartime and the peace conference itself; that of the 1920s and 1930s, spilling over into the mid-1950s; the German debate of the 1960s; and the historical work done outside Germany in the late 1960s and the decade of the 1970s. Let us examine each of these in turn.

The war had scarcely begun when each of the major powers sought to explain how it had come to pass. They did this less to explain their own policy than for two other reasons: first, to reassure their populations that they were fighting a defensive war and, second, to sway public opinion in neutral, or as yet uninvolved, countries. Groups of diplomatic dispatches were printed (many falsified, edited, or misdated) in publications called after the color of their jackets, "Red Book" or "Orange Book." These propaganda efforts later received a new stimulus when the Germans published captured Belgian documents which purportedly showed that Belgium had dealt with Britain and France before the war and that Germany was hence justified in violating Belgian neutrality in August 1914. After November 1917 the Bolsheviks released many of the pre-war tsarist documents and thereby placed the actions of the Triple Entente in a dubious light.

The emotionalism of the war, fueled by the human costs and the need to blame somebody, carried over to the peace conference. Although there was concern to understand who started the conflict, the leaders of the victorious powers—even Woodrow Wilson—were convinced that Berlin had been chiefly responsible. There was talk of prosecuting the German kaiser (who had conveniently fled to neutral Holland) and a mood of vengeance dominated the air. It was in this atmosphere that the victors appointed a commission to study (survey would be a better word) the causes of the war. With great haste and without access to the diplomatic records of any powers, the commission drafted a predictable report: Germany was blamed for the war and the other powers were absolved of the charges hurled against them during the war. Throughout the report ran the implicit assumption that a declarative statement was the equivalent of a historical conclusion (see "Report Presented to the Preliminary Peace Conference," page 1). Moreover, the report served as the basis for the famous "war guilt clause"—Article 231 of the Treaty of Versailles—that charged Germany and Austria-Hungary with causing the war. Further, the new German government, despite its fledgling status as a new democratic state, was forced to accept this historical indictment in the final peace treaty which was signed with irony and bitterness on June 28, 1919.

Almost immediately the German government moved to discredit and repudiate the Versailles "verdict." In doing so, the new regime launched an unprecedented effort that ultimately benefited all historians: they systematically began to publish their pre-1914 diplomatic documents and memoranda as *Die grosse Politik der europäischen Kabinette*. These appeared in forty volumes (sixty separate books) covering the years 1871 to 1914. While not complete and in some cases carefully selected, the documents made German foreign policy before 1914 seem less forbidding, less plotting, and less clever. At the same time, the German Foreign Office set up a quasi-scholarly journal, *Die Kriegschuldfrage (The War Guilt Question)*, later called the *Berliner Monatshefte*. Each issue of the journal carried articles and documents which hammered away at the theme of revising the Versailles Treaty. The revisionists' efforts had consistent support from the German political and economic leadership. All were intent—for political, moral, economic, and historical reasons—to cast doubt upon the quick judgments reached at the peace conference. Of those who joined the chorus none was more vehement, skilled, and successful than the former corporal and later tyrant, Adolf Hitler. Hitler's views on the origins of the

war (see page 5) formed part of his larger tirade in *Mein Kampf*, but they were not much different from those held by many Germans of all political persuasions; some, however, such as Erich Brandenburg (see page 7), were more moderate.

Nor were the German efforts without success. The new documentation necessitated a reconsideration of earlier views. Diligent researchers began to move away from the orthodox position of the wartime. During the mid-1920s in Britain, France, and especially the United States, the revisionist movement gained momentum. In this work there was a mixture of balanced historical investigation, ideological handwringing, and belated pangs over the wrongs done Germany by the peace settlement. Two selections from these revisionist historians are included in this volume: Harry Elmer Barnes, the more extreme publicist, presents a liberal view; Sidney B. Fay provides a more comprehensive historical analysis.

The publication of the German documents compelled the British and French to respond (without much enthusiasm, it might be added) with their own volumes of documents. The first British volume appeared in 1926; the first French volume in 1929, and later even the Soviet Union would publish some documents on tsarist foreign policy. The defeated Austrians added their own as well. The French and Belgian governments, moreover, copied the German in subsidizing a journal devoted to the coming of the war and designed, of course, to counter the calls for "revision" of the peace treaty. Thus, though no government systematically allowed scholars into its archives, within two decades after 1914 a major segment of the diplomatic exchanges were available to historians and scholars. In addition, by 1930 many of the leading protagonists on all sides had published memoirs or diaries that added evidence. To be sure, the existence of the diplomatic documents inevitably meant that the study focused more on diplomacy and strategy than on economic or domestic policies or even public opinion, but work in those areas did take place.

The flow of "revisionist writing" and

Hitler's political successes should not obscure the degree to which the orthodox position on 1914 remained dominant. The revisionist writing and historical arguments convinced one intellectual and social stratum, but for the wider public in France, Britain, and the United States "the Huns" remained responsible for 1914, and the emotions generated by reparations merely reinforced this view. It was also echoed in some equally thoughtful historical works, such as Bernadotte Schmitt's two-volume study, *The Coming of the War, 1914,* and G. P. Gooch's set of pen portraits, *Before the War.* This view about Germany's responsibility would, moreover, receive new adherents as Hitler's steady policy of opportunism and aggression unfolded during the late 1930s.

In the meantime an Italian newspaperman, Luigi Albertini, studied all the document volumes and set out to write a full account of the coming of the war. His three-volume work, published first in Italian in the early 1940s and then translated into English in the mid-1950s, is not easily excerpted, but this volume of readings does offer a summary of his views. Albertini reiterated—with many nuances and alterations—the Versailles opinion that the German and Austro-Hungarian governments had been chiefly responsible for the coming of the war. Yet while Albertini reflected a wide public and a certain scholarly opinion of the 1914 crisis, his views went largely unnoticed in the late 1940s and early 1950s. Indeed, when a group of French and German historians sought—as part of the European movement after 1945—to agree upon a statement about 1914, Albertini's assessment was noticeably not reflected in their conclusions. Instead they avoided laying precise blame or responsibility and talked rather of mutual contributions to the destruction of the peace.

Thus, when the decade of the 1950s ended, the debate on 1914 had expanded and become infinitely detailed and often tedious; yet it also remained much the same. The debate no longer focused on "guilt" but on "responsibility," and no longer on the responsibility of a single nation but of several nations. Also there were clear distinctions between the short- and long-term causes of the war and a strong belief that no leaders had excelled in their performances in the summer of 1914. On the whole, the revisionist views held by Fay dominated American academic circles; and a slightly more skeptical revisionism existed in Britain. For their part, the German historians and the German public in the West remained attached to their revisionist positions as developed and nurtured during the 1920s. Only the French remained convinced of their own innocence and of German culpability.

II

In 1961, almost a half-century later, much of this changed as the debate on 1914 took an abrupt new turn. The third distinct stage of the historiography of the war began. Before 1961 no prominent German historian (save for some hints here and there) had argued in print that the verdict of Versailles was essentially correct. In the late 1920s Eckart Kehr had raised troublesome issues, but his early death cut short a thorough study; another German historian, Hermann Kantorowicz, had his views effectively suppressed in the 1920s when he could find no publisher. Thus Fritz Fischer's blockbuster, *Griff nach der Weltmacht,* hit hard when it appeared in 1961. The study's essential focus was upon Germany's expansionist policy during World War I itself and the wide support it enjoyed among military and civilian circles.

These points were, however, nearly overshadowed by his preliminary chapter on the coming of the war. Not only did Fischer accuse Germany of responsibility for the war, but he also stridently showed how the civilian leadership (and especially Chancellor Bethmann Hollweg), as well as the military, were prepared to risk conflict. If many of his arguments did not appear novel (certainly not to careful readers of Albertini), their appearance in West Germany shocked many of Fischer's contemporaries and older historians particularly. For nearly a decade thereafter Fischer, aided by a series of younger German historians (most notably Imanuel Geiss), propounded the thesis of German responsibility, of German recklessness, and of Germany's calculated moves to war. From the Fischer school came articles, collections of documents, and monographs. Then in 1969 the Hamburg professor published a second work, *Krieg der Illusionen (The War of Illusions)*, in which he examined German foreign policy from 1911 through the outbreak of the war. In this study the earlier arguments were linked with more detailed background and the aggressiveness of German policy was established more conclusively (see excerpt page 25).

The writings of the Fischer school have had three related impacts. First, they divided much of German historical scholarship in the 1960s: in part along age lines, in part along ideological lines, in part along methodological and conceptual lines. Older historians such as Gerhard Ritter and Karl D. Erdmann charged Fischer with creating a new war guilt thesis; others, less tolerant, charged him with opening issues suitably left closed or forgotten. Still others praised the breath of fresh air that Fischer brought, while deploring his old-fashioned history, his easy historical determinism, and his failure to describe how institutions function, especially the connection between ideas and political action. Among the historians of the latter camp is Wolfgang Mommsen, a member of the famous German family of historians and a tolerant critic of Fischer (see "War as a Product of Governmental Instability," page 44). Now, nearly two decades after Fischer's initial foray, one can confidently state that he changed both the landscape and the character of German historical writing about Wilhelminian Germany. And this influence was not confined to West Germany; it helped to shape much of the tone and substance of the work undertaken by East German historians like Fritz Klein and his associates at the *Zentralinstitut für Geschichte* of the *Akademie der Wissenschaft*. If the Fischer school has concentrated excessive attention (and in turn responsibil-

ity) on German policy, it has nonetheless pressed West German scholarship into a broader, less statist view of history. The results have contributed to a productive historical dialectic.

But Fischer's contribution has had a second quality as well. He opened unexpected vistas on the extent and value of new archival sources. He and his associates were among the first to examine the archival record in a way that no historian could have done before 1939. In fact, Germany's second defeat accelerated the opening of some materials conveniently captured by the Western powers, while it also convinced many that the pre-1914 world was of only academic interest. Subsequently Fischer's use of papers from the German Foreign Ministry, the German navy, and private collections produced voluminous details that recast many of the questions about the background and origins of World War I. Moreover, mere access triggered new questions, not least about the shadowy world of high finance, economic elites, and relations between ministers and senior policymakers. Thus Fischer challenged both the previous, orthodox German view that Berlin was not unilaterally responsible for the war and did so in a fashion that pushed the entire discussion away from diplomacy into the realm of economic and social issues.

Finally, Fischer framed an unrelenting indictment of German policy. If the central theme of much of his work—Germany's responsibility for the 1914 war—struck few new notes outside Germany, his argumentation of that proposition did. Germany wanted the war, so Fischer argued, because the German political and social leadership saw in a war a chance to recoup its ebbing power and prestige. The German military, especially after 1912, looked tirelessly for an opportunity to go to war before Russia became too strong. Fischer even charged that a Crown Council in December 1912 deliberately plotted a course for war, not unlike the course Hitler charted at the so-called Hossbach conference in late 1937. In this premeditated policy the British position was crucial; Bethmann Hollweg worked to separate Britain from its ententes with France and Russia. Through naval negotiations, discussions on colonial and commercial issues, and a general diminution in name calling, the German chancellor, so Fischer wrote, hoped to convince Britain to remain neutral if war came. Further, Fischer argued that in the summer of 1914 Berlin did in fact believe that Britain would stand aside, especially since the war would start over a Balkan issue. Above all, Berlin was willing to take a calculated risk on Britain's decision.

Not only these views, but the stridency behind them shaped Fischer's writings and that of his principal students. The German government of Bismarck and then Wilhelm II was expansionist; its foreign policy was almost solely a product of domestic political needs; its leadership alone among European leaders wanted war, after 1912 worked toward it, and actively sought it in the summer of 1914. To buttress this set of accusations Fischer also stressed the growing influence after 1912 of the army leadership (that of the navy actually declined) though he did not explore the structure of this influence with any precision. Repeatedly Fischer argued his central point on the coming of the war: the unilateral, dominating influence of Germany. With Fischer there is little room for other states or other leaders, or for the simple play of miscalculation, foibles, and ambitions. Pre-1914 Germany had more than enough for all.

Outside Germany, Fischer's impact can be described as spotty. For many historians his 1961 indictment added little that was new save the fact that a German made it. For others, especially after the 1969 volume, the range of new argumentation, new evidence, and new stress on the relationship between domestic and foreign policy represented brilliant insights into German policy both before and during 1914. Readable, pungent, and less rambling than Albertini, Fischer (and Geiss) drove home the more orthodox views of the interwar period—about German responsibility for the events that brought the Great War. On the whole most Anglo-Saxon writers accepted Fischer's general conclusions about German responsi-

bility, but were less convinced of a German plan for war and were uncertain about the part played by Chancellor Bethmann Hollweg. Moreover, many objected that Germany did not exist alone in the international system and that its foreign policy had to be understood in the context of the broader diplomatic system. In any event, Fischer's impact, echoed by Volker Berghahn and others, represented a significant historiographical milestone; the understanding of 1914 was thoroughly enriched by the intensity of the debate touched off in Germany during the 1960s.

III

While discussion raged in West Germany, scholars in Britain, the United States and, to a far less extent, France, worked on problems that fed into a different but also new understanding of 1914. Indeed, possibly the more interesting questions were posed by these historians, though not always in the encyclopedic fashion of Fischer or with his emotional impact. These historians also helped to add a comparative, multi-state dimension to events before 1914. And their efforts can be said to have moved the historiography of July 1914 into still another phase—the current one—and that phase appears likely to remain stable for a decade or more.

One of the most suggestive of these analyses dealt with the unspoken assumptions that both the public and the policymakers took into the 1914 crisis. How did they regard the use of force? What part did Social Darwinist thought play in their readiness to accept violence? How were nationalist movements regarded? What images of the future of the Habsburg monarchy did policymakers possess? James Joll's article "The Unspoken Assumptions" (see page 52) asked these kinds of questions. If scholars have not yet fully grappled in depth with them, nor indeed engaged in any systematic, psychological approach to a major figure of the July crisis, an understanding of such approaches will doubtless prove indispensable to a more complete understanding of the plunge into war.

One early effort that followed Joll's admonition came from the pen of the Columbia University historian Fritz Stern in his essay on Chancellor Bethmann Hollweg (see page 36). In this selection the chancellor's views, attitudes, and sense of political responsibility are examined. What emerges is a portrait of a complex political leader atop an uncertain political structure, a man afflicted with self-doubts and worried about the future of Germany and its place in European politics. These doubts the deaths at Sarajevo merely intensified. What, for example, would be the future of the Habsburg monarchy with the fifty-year-old heir apparent dead, an eighty-four-year-old monarch on the throne, and the new heir apparent only twenty-six? Why were the Russians playing so dangerously in the Balkan maelstrom? Would a striking diplomatic triumph restore confidence to the Triple Alliance? Stern allows the reader to glimpse the difficulties that any senior official confronts: Is this the time to act? How much information do I possess? How valid is it? How will the decision or the lack of a decision be interpreted by others? And he reminds the reader that all of this takes place in a situation of confusion in which the statesman must also make other decisions, so that a significant decision can be taken almost imperceptibly. If Stern's view of Bethmann Hollweg differs from and is more charitable than that of Fischer, both assessments stress the chancellor's central place in the July crisis.

The comparative perspective—that of seeing German policy in the context of the diplomacy, strategy, and ambitions of other powers—has been facilitated by the extensive work on Britain in the years before 1914. Leading much of this reassessment has been Zara Steiner, whose study of the British Foreign Office, which appeared in 1969, opened new perspectives on bureaucracy and the making of Britain's anti-German policy. Other writers, including Nicholas d'Ombrain, John Gooch, Paul Halpern, and the editor of this volume, have contributed to an appreciation of the strategic calculations that saw

Britain first turn to a continental diplomacy and then to a continental strategy. The work on French policy has been less extensive, apart from the publications of Christopher Andrew on Théophile Delcassé and French imperialism, but that by F. R. Bridge, Norman Stone, Joachim Remak, and Paul Schroeder on Austria-Hungary has necessitated an upward valuation of the tenacity and political durability of the Danubian monarchy. Extensive new work on the conspiracy behind the shots fired at Sarajevo has shown the Serbian actions (and complicity) more starkly. What emerges when the studies are taken together is a world of international politics at once more complicated, more interactive, and less unilateral than the Fischer view would permit or encourage. At the same time most of the work warns, as does Zara Steiner's most recent study (see page 64), against the risks of attempting to apply any one "explanatory model" on the broader sphere of international politics. Instead, a more synthetic approach that balances external and internal developments, that allows for human frailty, that sees linkages between external crises and state responses, and that appreciates the complexities of decision making is a more effective, possibly a more lasting, way to explain the events that brought war in 1914.

American scholars have contributed numerous articles and monographs in one area: the effort to quantify the study of international politics using the 1914 crisis as the illustrative example. Guided by Robert C. North of Stanford University, this group has coded the diplomatic documents, designed computer programs that seek to isolate key variables, and tried to identify corrective steps that—if taken—might reduce the chances of a repeat of 1914. On the whole, these efforts have been judged—especially by historians—as only modestly successful. The principal weaknesses have been an excessive reliance on diplomatic documents that tell only part of the story, the difficulty of moving from long-term to immediate causes, and a fixation on Anglo-German relations rather than the broader canvas of European international politics.

Nonetheless, this work has led to a vast accumulation of new data, required more precision from historians in their use of terms, and helped to isolate major choices as they may have appeared to the policymakers. These gains are in part reflected in the systematic, analytical piece by L. L. Farrar which concludes this book of readings.

IV

Despite the passage of six decades, historical interest in the outbreak of World War I remains intense. Many of the major issues have been defined, elucidated, and resolved. But many more remain unaddressed, even unexplored. Nowhere, for example, is this more evident than with Russian foreign policy both before and during the July crisis. Although the Bolsheviks released some diplomatic documents in the 1920s and 1930s, Soviet historians have not been allowed much access to the archival materials, and there is scant research on pre-1914 tsarist foreign policy. Nor have the Communist governments in eastern Europe encouraged such exploration into their pre-1914 history, though there have been some major and helpful exceptions (Yugoslavia in particular). But eastern Europe is not the only place where gaps exist. Much work is needed on the French political system, on French policymaking, and on the exact nature of alliance relationships between Paris and St. Petersburg. Present works on Italian foreign policy do little to advance the understanding beyond what Albertini wrote in the early 1940s. By contrast the Habsburg monarchy, central to any understanding of the start of the local war in 1914, is receiving new attention and in turn forcing anew a recognition of the limits of Fischer's interpretations. Only the Anglo-German relationship and the many topics associated with it may be said to have reached a level that permits effective synthesis and generalization.

If sizable gaps remain for some of the pre-1914 governments, there are equally large gaps in the topics covered. The diplomatic record is generally defined, as are many of the strategic issues. But decision making, the role of the intelligence systems, the actual operation of many of the governments, the influence and part played by high finance, and the entire area of intellectual and political assumptions—all of these require detailed and comparative investigation. So also does the development of that psychological feeling—so widely shared throughout Europe and affirmed by the noisy crowds in August 1914—that led the public to welcome the prospect of war. There is much evidence for Zara Steiner's observation: "Europe was deeply ready for war." But why this dangerous atmosphere? Can it occur again? These are crucial questions of continuing relevance and importance.

GLOSSARY OF NAMES

Aehrenthal, Alois, Baron (later Count) Lexa: Austro-Hungarian Foreign Minister, 1906-1912.

Asquith, Herbert Henry: British Prime Minister, 1908-1916.

Berchtold, Leopold, Count: Austro-Hungarian Foreign Minister, 1912-1915.

Bethmann Hollweg, Theobald von: German Chancellor, 1909-1917.

Bilinski, Leon von: Austro-Hungarian Common Finance Minister with responsibility for the administration of Bosnia-Herzegovina, 1912-1915.

Cambon, Jules: French ambassador to Berlin, 1907-1914.

Cambon, Paul: French ambassador to London, 1898-1920.

Churchill, Winston S.: First Lord of the Admiralty, 1911-1915.

Conrad von Hötzendorf, Franz, Baron (later Count): Chief of the Austro-Hungarian General Staff, 1906-1911, 1912-1917.

Crowe, Sir Eyre: Assistant Undersecretary of State, British Foreign Office, 1912-1920.

Delcassé, Théophile: French Foreign Minister, 1898-1905, French ambassador to St. Petersburg, 1913-1914.

Dimitrievic, Dragutin (code name "Apis"): Head of Serbian military intelligence; major figure in the Black Hand.

Forgach, Johann, Count: First Section Chief, Austro-Hungarian Foreign Ministry, 1913-1917.

Franz Ferdinand: Austro-Hungarian archduke and heir to the throne.

Franz Joseph: Emperor of Austria and King of Hungary, 1848-1916.

Grey, Sir Edward (later Viscount Grey of Fallodon): British Foreign Secretary, 1905-1916.

Hoyos, Alexander, Count: *Chef de cabinet,* Austro-Hungarian Foreign Ministry, 1912-1917.

Isvolsky, Alexander: Russian Foreign Minister, 1906-1910: Russian ambassador to Paris, 1910-1917.

Jagow, Gottlieb von: German Foreign Minister, 1913-1916.

Lichnowsky, Prince von: German ambassador to London, 1912-1914.

Lloyd George, David: British Chancellor of the Exchequer, 1908-1915.

Moltke, General Helmut von: Chief of the German General Staff, 1906-1914.

Morley, John (later Viscount Morley of Blackburn): Lord President of the Council, 1910-1914.

Nicolson, Sir Arthur (later Lord Carnock): Brisith ambassador to St. Petersburg, 1906-1910; Permanent Undersecretary of the Foreign Office, 1910-1916.

Paléologue, Maurice: French ambassador to St. Petersburg, 1914-1917.

Pasić, Nikola: Serbian Prime Minister and Minister of Foreign Affairs, 1906-1918.

Poincaré, Raymond: Prime Minister and also Minister for Foreign Affairs, 1912-1913; President of the French Republic, 1913-1920.

Pourtalès, Friedrich von, Count: German ambassador to St. Petersburg, 1907-1914.

Princip, Gavrilo: Bosnian assassin of Franz Ferdinand and his wife, Sophie.

Rathenau, Walther: Director of *Allgemeine Elektrizitäts-Gesellschaft* (AEG) and country neighbor of Bethmann Hollweg.

Riezler, Kurt: German publicist; aide, confidant of Bethmann Hollweg.

San Giuliano, Antonino, Marquis of: Italian Minister for Foreign Affairs, 1910-1916.

Sazonov, Sergei: Russian Foreign Minister, 1910-1916.

Schlieffen, General Alfred von: Chief of the German General Staff, 1891-1905.

Sukhomilnov, General V. A.: Russian Minister for War, 1909-1915.

Szögyeny-Marich, Laszlo, Count: Austro-Hungarian ambassador to Berlin, 1892-1914.

Tirpitz, Admiral Alfred von: German Naval Minister, 1898-1916.

Tisza, Stephan, Count: Hungarian Prime Minister, 1913-1917.

Tschirschky und Bogendorff, Heinrich von: German ambassador to Vienna, 1907-1916.

Viviani, René: French Premier, 1914-1915; also Minister for Foreign Affairs, June 13-August 3, 1914.

Zimmermann, Arthur: German Undersecretary for Foreign Affairs, 1911-1916.

CHRONOLOGICAL SURVEY

1870-1871	Franco-Prussian War: German Empire emerges from French defeat and annexes French provinces of Alsace and Lorraine, poisoning Franco-German relations thereafter
1877-1878	Russo-Turkish war: Russia makes large gains in the Balkans under the Treaty of San Stefano
1878	Congress of Berlin overthrows San Stefano settlement and readjusts Balkan balance: Austria-Hungary gains right to "administer" Bosnia-Herzegovina
1879	Austria-Hungary and Germany sign alliance treaty
1882	Italy joins the Austro-German alliance; it becomes the Triple Alliance
1894	Franco-Russian alliance agreements exchanged
1898	Fashoda crisis between Britain and France; Tirpitz gets German naval law
1899	First Hague Peace Conference
1899-1902	Anglo-Boer War
1902	Anglo-Japanese alliance
1904	Russo-Japanese War; Anglo-French entente
1905	First Moroccan crisis
1906	Anglo-French military conversations; launching of first *Dreadnought*
1907	Second Hague Conference; Anglo-Russian entente
1908	September: Aehrenthal and Isvolsky meet at Buchlau
	October: Austria-Hungary announces annexation of Bosnia-Herzegovina; crisis ensues
1911	Second Moroccan crisis over Agadir; Italy attacks Turkey in Tripoli
1912	February: Haldane mission and Anglo-German naval talks
	March: formation of Balkan League under Russian sponsorship

October: outbreak of first Balkan war
Russia keeps third-year troops on active duty; Austria-Hungary mobilizes some troops

December: German crown council allegedly plots war
Austria-Hungary decides not to attack Serbia

1913   May: Austria-Hungary issues ultimatum to Montenegro over Skutari; Treaty of London ends first Balkan war

June: second Balkan war begins

August: Treaty of Bucharest ends second Balkan war

November-December: Russo-German tension over Liman von Sanders affair

1914   March: Russo-German press war

June: Kaiser Wilhelm II visits Archduke Franz Ferdinand

June 28: Assassination of Archduke Franz Ferdinand and wife Sophie at Sarajevo

July 5: Hoyos mission to Berlin; Austria-Hungary receives "blank check" for action against Serbia

July 7: Habsburg Common Council favors war with Serbia: Hungarian Premier Tisza opposes

July 14: Tisza agrees to war on stipulation of no additional territory to Habsburg monarchy

July 19: Habsburg Common Council approves terms of ultimatum

July 20-23: French President Poincaré and Premier Viviani in St. Petersburg; French reaffirm their diplomatic support of Russia

July 23: Austria-Hungary gives 48-hour ultimatum to Serbia

July 25: Serbian reply does not accept demand for an outside (Habsburg) investigation of conspiracy;
Serbia orders mobilization;
Russia takes some steps preliminary to mobilization

July 26: Grey proposes mediation; it is rejected by Vienna

July 28: Austria-Hungary partially mobilizes and declares war on Serbia; Halt in Belgrade plan suggested; Vienna later rejects it

July 29: scattered Austro-Hungarian shelling of Serbian territory; Germany attempts to win British neutrality

July 30: Russia orders general mobilization; Britain rebuffs German overtures on neutrality

July 31: Germany declares state of threatening danger of war: demands that Russia cease its mobilization; Austria-Hungary orders general mobilization

August 1: France refuses to bow to German demands of neutrality in event of Russo-German war:
France and Germany mobilize;
Germany declares war on Russia

August 2: British cabinet gives limited assurance to France on defense of its northern coasts;
Germany invades Luxembourg

August 3: Germany invades Belgium;
Germany declares war on France

August 4: Britain declares war on Germany

August 6: Austria-Hungary declares war on Russia

CONFLICT OF OPINION

"The Allied and Associated Governments affirm and Germany accepts the responsibility of Germany and her allies for causing all the loss and damage to which the Allies and Associated Governments and their nationals have been subjected as a consequence of the war imposed upon them by the aggression of Germany and her allies."

—ARTICLE 231 OF THE TREATY OF VERSAILLES

"The struggle of the year 1914 was not forced on the masses—no, by the living God—it was desired by the whole people."

—ADOLF HITLER

"In estimating the order of guilt of the various countries we may safely say that the only direct and immediate responsibility for the World War falls upon Serbia, France and Russia, with the guilt equally distributed. Next in order—far below France and Russia—would come Austria, though she never desired a general European war. Finally, we should place Germany and England as tied for last place, both being opposed to war in the 1914 crisis."

—HARRY ELMER BARNES

"Nevertheless, a European War broke out. Why? Because in each country political and military leaders did certain things which led to mobilizations and declarations of war, or failed to do certain things which might have prevented them. In this sense, all the European countries, in a greater or less degree, were responsible. One must abandon the dictum of the Versailles Treaty that Germany and her allies were solely responsible."

—SIDNEY B. FAY

"While the German government was determined from early July 1914 onwards to use this favourable opportunity for a war against France and Russia, the government of Vienna had decided on firm steps against Serbia but was looking for ways and means to avoid a military intervention by Russia. . . .These almost timorous attempts to justify the delay show to what extent the Austro-Hungarian politicians felt pushed into a war against Serbia by the German government."

—FRITZ FISCHER

"It is incontrovertible that Bethmann consciously risked a world war, but there is no evidence that he did so in order to establish German hegemony. It is naive and excessively rationalistic to suppose that aggression must spring from lust of conquest. Fear, too, impels aggressive action."

—FRITZ STERN

"In the last analysis, we may conclude, the causes of the First World War must be sought not in the blunders and miscalculations of the governments alone, but in the fact that Germany's governmental system, as well as Austria-Hungary's and Russia's, was no longer adequate in the face of rapid social change and the steady advance of mass politics."

—WOLFGANG MOMMSEN

"The sense of inevitability and the sense of relief, as the crisis mounted and as war came. . .is also due, I suggest, to the fact that by 1914 the ideas of both Darwin and of Nietzsche had become widely assimilated, so that there were many people in Europe, both among rulers and ruled, who thought of life in terms of the struggle for survival, or who were looking for an opportunity to transcend the limitations of their ordinary lives and to find a new set of values in what they believed would be a new and enriching experience."

—JAMES JOLL

"All rejected diplomatic defeat since it implied the price of military defeat without the possibility of victory. War at least implied the possibility of victory as well as defeat. Thus diplomatic victory was impossible because diplomatic defeat was inconceivable, whereas war was conceivable. Consequently when a choice seemed imperative, war became imperative."

—L. L. FARRAR

I. THE INITIAL DEBATE OVER WAR GUILT

Commission on the Responsibility
of the Authors of the War
and on the Enforcement of Penalties

REPORT PRESENTED TO THE
PRELIMINARY PEACE CONFERENCE

A major question for the peacemakers after World War I was who had been responsible or, to put it more critically, who was guilty for the outbreak of war. In January 1919 the victorious powers created a fifteen-member commission to examine the question. After an initial report in late March, a final report was subsequently adopted (with some amendments) by the entire conference on May 6, 1919. This early "historical" assessment served to justify the inclusion of the famous war guilt clause—Article 231—in the final peace treaty. That article, which made the responsibility still more precise and sweeping, stated: "The Allied and Associated Governments affirm and Germany accepts the responsibility of Germany and her allies for causing all the loss and damage to which the Allied and Associated Governments and their nationals have been subjected as a consequence of the war imposed upon them by the aggression of Germany and her allies." For the victorious peacemakers there was no question about who caused the war or what history would show about the events of July-August 1914. For the defeated states war guilt would become a historical, moral, diplomatic, and political issue of supreme importance.

In reading this selection note the issues of causation, historical accuracy, and perspective that are raised—either implicitly or explicitly— by the 1919 report.

O N THE question of the responsibility of the authors of the war, the Commission, after having examined a number of official documents relating to the origin of the World War, and to the violations of neutrality and of frontiers which accompanied its inception, has determined that the responsibility for it lies wholly upon the Powers which declared war in pursuance of a policy of aggression, the concealment of which gives to the origin of this war the character of a dark conspiracy against the peace of Europe.

This responsibility rests first on Germany and Austria, secondly on Turkey and Bulgaria. The responsibility is made all the graver by reason of the violation by Germany and Austria of the neutrality of

From "Report presented to the Preliminary Peace Conference by the Commission on the Responsibility of the Authors of the War and on the Enforcement of Penalties," in *German White Book Concerning the Responsibility of the Authors of the War*, trans. Carnegie Endowment for International Peace (New York: Oxford University Press, 1924), pp. 15-21. Used by permission of the Carnegie Endowment for International Peace. Footnotes omitted in this and subsequent selections.

Belgium and Luxemburg, which they themselves had guaranteed. It is increased, with regard to both France and Serbia, by the violation of their frontiers before the declaration of war.

Many months before the crisis of 1914 the German Emperor had ceased to pose as the champion of peace. Naturally believing in the overwhelming superiority of his Army, he openly showed his enmity towards France. General von Moltke said to the King of the Belgians: "This time the matter must be settled." In vain the King protested. The Emperor and his Chief of Staff remained no less fixed in their attitude.

On the 28th of June, 1914, occurred the assassination at Sarajevo of the heir apparent of Austria. "It is the act of a little group of madmen," said Francis Joseph. The act, committed as it was by a subject of Austria-Hungary on Austro-Hungarian territory, could in no wise compromise Serbia, which very correctly expressed its condolences and stopped public rejoicings in Belgrade. If the Government of Vienna thought that there was any Serbian complicity, Serbia was ready to seek out the guilty parties. But this attitude failed to satisfy Austria and still less Germany, who, after their first astonishment had passed, saw in this royal and national misfortune a pretext to initiate war.

At Potsdam a "decisive consultation" took place on the 5th of July, 1914. Vienna and Berlin decided upon this plan: "Vienna will send to Belgrade a very emphatic ultimatum with a very short limit of time."

The Bavarian Minister, von Lerchenfeld, said in a confidential dispatch dated the 18th of July, 1914, the facts stated in which have never been officially denied: "It is clear that Serbia cannot accept the demands, which are inconsistent with the dignity of an independent state." Count Lerchenfeld reveals in this report that, at the time it was made, the ultimatum to Serbia had been jointly decided upon by the Governments of Berlin and Vienna; that they were waiting to send it until President Poincaré and Mr. Viviani should have left for St. Petersburg; and that no illusions were cherished, either

at Berlin or Vienna, as to the consequences which this threatening measure would involve. It was perfectly well known that war would be the result.

The Bavarian Minister explains, moreover, that the only fear of the Berlin Government was that Austria-Hungary might hesitate and draw back at the last minute, and that on the other hand Serbia, on the advice of France and Great Britain, might yield to the pressure put upon her. Now, "the Berlin Government considers that war is necessary." Therefore, it gave full powers to Count Berchtold, who instructed the Ballplatz on the 18th of July, 1914, to negotiate with Bulgaria to induce her to enter into an alliance and to participate in the war.

In order to mask this understanding, it was arranged that the Emperor should go for a cruise in the North Sea, and that the Prussian Minister of War should go for a holiday, so that the Imperial Government might pretend that events had taken it completely by surprise.

Austria suddenly sent Serbia an ultimatum that she had carefully prepared in such a way as to make it impossible to accept. Nobody could be deceived; "the whole world understands that this ultimatum means war." According to Mr. Sazonoff, "Austria-Hungary wanted to devour Serbia."

Mr. Sazonoff asked Vienna for an extension of the short time limit of forty-eight hours given by Austria to Serbia for the most serious decision in its history. Vienna refused the demand. On the 24th and 25th of July, England and France multiplied their efforts to persuade Serbia to satisfy the Austro-Hungarian demands. Russia threw in her weight on the side of conciliation.

Contrary to the expectation of Austria-Hungary and Germany, Serbia yielded. She agreed to all the requirements of the ultimatum, subject to the single reservation that, in the judicial inquiry which she would commence for the purpose of seeking out the guilty parties, the participation of Austrian officials would be kept within the limits assigned by international law. "If the

Austro-Hungarian Government is not satisfied with this," Serbia declared she was ready "to submit to the decision of the Hague Tribunal."

"A quarter of an hour before the expiration of the time limit," at 5:45 on the 25th, Mr. Pashitch, the Serbian Minister for Foreign Affairs, delivered this reply to Baron Giesl, the Austro-Hungarian Minister.

On Mr. Pashitch's return to his own office he found awaiting him a letter from Baron Giesl saying that he was not satisfied with the reply. At 6:30 the latter had left Belgrade, and even before he had arrived at Vienna, the Austro-Hungarian Government had handed his passports to Mr. Yovanovitch, the Serbian Minister, and had prepared thirty-three mobilization proclamations, which were published on the following morning in the *Budapesti Kozlöni,* the official gazette of the Hungarian Government. On the 27th Sir Maurice de Bunsen telegraphed to Sir Edward Grey: "This country has gone wild with joy at the prospect of war with Serbia." At midday on the 28th Austria declared war on Serbia. On the 29th the Austrian army commenced the bombardment of Belgrade and made its dispositions to cross the frontier.

The reiterated suggestions of the Entente Powers with a view to finding a peaceful solution of the dispute only produced evasive replies on the part of Berlin or promises of intervention with the Government of Vienna without any effectual steps being taken.

On the 24th of July Russia and England asked that the Powers should be granted a reasonable delay in which to work in concert for the maintenance of peace. Germany did not join in this request.

On the 25th of July Sir Edward Grey proposed mediation by four Powers (England, France, Italy and Germany). France and Italy immediately gave their concurrence. Germany refused, alleging that it was not a question of mediation but of arbitration, as the conference of the four Powers was called to make proposals, not to decide.

On the 26th of July Russia proposed to negotiate directly with Austria. Austria refused.

On the 27th of July England proposed a European conference. Germany refused.

On the 29th of July Sir Edward Grey asked the Wilhelmstrasse to be good enough to "suggest any method by which the influence of the four Powers could be used together to prevent a war between Austria and Russia." She was asked herself to say what she desired. Her reply was evasive.

On the same day, the 29th of July, the Czar dispatched to the Emperor William II a telegram suggesting that the Austro-Serbian problem should be submitted to the Hague Tribunal. This suggestion received no reply. This important telegram does not appear in the German White Book. It was made public by the Petrograd *Official Gazette* (January, 1915).

The Bavarian Legation, in a report dated the 31st of July, declared its conviction that the efforts of Sir Edward Grey to preserve peace would not hinder the march of events.

As early as the 21st of July German mobilization had commenced by the recall of a certain number of classes of the reserve, then of German officers in Switzerland, and finally of the Metz garrison on the 25th of July. On the 26th of July the German fleet was called back from Norway.

The Entente did not relax its conciliatory efforts, but the German Government systematically brought all its attempts to naught. When Austria consented for the first time on the 31st of July to discuss the contents of the Serbian note with the Russian Government and the Austro-Hungarian Ambassador received orders to "converse" with the Russian Minister of Foreign Affairs, Germany made any negotiation impossible by sending her ultimatum to Russia. Prince Lichnowsky wrote that "a hint from Berlin would have been enough to decide Count Berchtold to content himself with a diplomatic success and to declare that he was satisfied with the Serbian reply, but this hint was not given. *On the contrary they went forward towards war.*"

On the 1st of August the German Emperor addressed a telegram to the King of England containing the following sentence: "The troops on my frontier are, at this moment, being kept back by telegraphic and telephonic orders from crossing the French frontier." Now, war was not declared till two days after that date, and as the German mobilization orders were issued on that same day, the 1st of August, it follows that, as a matter of fact, the German Army had been mobilized and concentrated in pursuance of previous orders.

The attitude of the Entente nevertheless remained still to the very end so conciliatory that, at the very time at which the German fleet was bombarding Libau, Nicholas II gave his word of honor to William II that Russia would not undertake any aggressive action during the *pourparlers,* and that when the German troops commenced their march across the French frontier Mr. Viviani telegraphed to all the French Ambassadors "we must not stop working for accommodation."

On the 3rd of August Mr. von Schoen went to the Quai d'Orsay with the declaration of war against France. Lacking a real cause of complaint, Germany alleged, in her declaration of war, that bombs had been dropped by French airplanes in various districts in Germany. This statement was entirely false. Moreover, it was either later admitted to be so or no particulars were ever furnished by the German Government.

Moreover, in order to be manifestly above reproach, France was careful to withdraw her troops ten kilometers from the German frontier. Notwithstanding this precaution, numerous officially established violations of French territory preceded the declaration of war.

The provocation was so flagrant that Italy, herself a member of the Triple Alliance, did not hesitate to declare that in view of the aggressive character of the war the *casus foederis* ceased to apply.

Editor's Observations

The preliminary "Report" touches upon a number of issues and problems that recur repeatedly in all discussions of the origins of World War I. Because they do recur, a number of them are listed below to serve as a study guide or organizer for the reader's use with the remaining selections. Naturally, these are not the only questions to consider, but they do form an initial list. (For convenience, the questions are listed in the order in which they appear in—or are suggested by—the "Report.")

1. Which, how many and whose official documents had been examined by the Committee? Had it had access to the records of any government, or only the documents thus far published?

2. What was the impact of the German violation of Belgian neutrality (which all the major powers had guaranteed in 1839) upon public opinion, upon the British decision for war, and upon wartime propaganda?

3. What was the nature, character, and strength of the "policy of aggression" which the Central Powers had secretly pursued? Was it secret? Had the Germans been plotting the outbreak of the war for "many months?"

4. Were there both short- and long-term causes of the war, issues not related to the crisis of 1914 itself? Does the report mention any long-term causes of the war?

5. What was the role of German militarism in the coming of the war? Was it different from the militarism and navalism of the other powers, or of the victors?

6. Were the conspirators at Sarajevo really "madmen" or actually Bosnian nationalists with connections to the Serbian government? Did the Serbian government make any effort to trace the conspiracy?

7. Did the Sarajevo assassinations provide the pretext for the Habsburg govern-

ment to act, for the German government to act, for both to act, for neither?

8. What role did the conferences of July 5, 1914, between the senior German officials and members of the Habsburg embassy play in the coming of the war and in giving the "blank check" to Vienna?

9. Did Vienna frame the ultimatum so that it would be rejected? Was Berlin consulted in the drafting?

10. Did the governments in Berlin and Vienna deliberately deceive the other capitals about their plans in the summer of 1914?

11. Why did the Habsburgs fail to extend the deadline for the ultimatum? Did the Triple Entente powers counsel patience and compromise on Serbia?

12. Did Serbia actually accept the operative and most significant parts of the Austro-Hungarian ultimatum?

13. How extensive were the Austro-Hungarian measures prior to, and just after, the expiration of the deadline on July 25, 1914?

14. What impact did German and Austro-Hungarian failure to mediate have on the path to war? Was Paris or St. Petersburg more willing to negotiate?

15. Did Germany act dangerously on July 31 when it blocked further negotiation between St. Petersburg and Vienna, or was it merely responding to the fact of Russia's general mobilization of July 30 which is not mentioned by the preliminary "Report?"

16. What was the nature of the border incidents? Did they play any part in the major decisions by the allies and entente partners?

17. Was the Italian decision to remain neutral a reaction to the origins of the war or to the expectation of gains that might be made subsequently from a more timely entry?

Adolf Hitler

A GERMAN REBUTTAL

No historian's view of the July 1914 crisis has ever enjoyed the currency of that written by an erstwhile German political agitator in 1924. Penned while Hitler was imprisoned for the aborted Beer Hall Putsch of 1923 in Munich, the selection reflects deep animosity toward the Habsburgs, condemnation of Germany's earlier failure to act, and concern about Serbian agitation.

Hitler, born a Habsburg citizen in 1889, later migrated to Munich in April 1913. In February 1914 he was recalled to Austria for military service, only to be declared "unfit for combatant and auxiliary duties" and allowed to return to Munich. In August 1914 he appealed to King Ludwig III of Bavaria to be allowed to join the Bavarian army (a part of the

From Adolf Hitler, *Mein Kampf*, trans. Ralph Manheim, published by Houghton Mifflin Company, pp. 158-161. Copyright 1943 and © renewed by Houghton Mifflin. In London, published by Hutchinson Publishing Group, Ltd. Reprinted by permission of the publishers.

German army); the King agreed and Hitler's service began on August 16. After the war, Hitler joined the fledgling Nazi movement and by 1930 managed to convert it into a major German political organization. In January 1933—by entirely legal means—he became Chancellor of Germany; within months, he was a *de facto* dictator. Of all the revisionists' writings about the origins of World War I, Hitler's were the most influential—and ultimately the most devastating.

WHEN THE news of the murder of Archduke Francis Ferdinand arrived in Munich (I happened to be sitting at home and heard of it only vaguely), I was at first seized with worry that the bullets may have been shot from the pistols of German students, who, out of indignation at the heir apparent's continuous work of Slavization, wanted to free the German people from this internal enemy. What the consequence of this would have been was easy to imagine: a new wave of persecutions which would now have been "justified" and "explained" in the eyes of the whole world. But when, soon afterward, I heard the names of the supposed assassins, and moreover read that they had been identified as Serbs, a light shudder began to run through me at this vengeance of inscrutable Destiny.

The greatest friend of the Slavs had fallen beneath the bullets of Slavic fanatics.

Anyone with constant occasion in the last years to observe the relation of Austria to Serbia could not for a moment be in doubt that a stone had been set rolling whose course could no longer be arrested.

Those who today shower the Viennese government with reproaches on the form and content of the ultimatum it issued, do it an injustice. No other power in the world could have acted differently in the same situation and the same position. At her southeastern border Austria possessed an inexorable and mortal enemy who at shorter and shorter intervals kept challenging the monarchy and would never have left off until the moment favorable for the shattering of the Empire had arrived. There was reason to fear that this would occur at the latest with the death of the old Emperor; by then perhaps the old monarchy would no longer be in a position to offer any serious resistance. In the last few years the state had been so bound up with the person of Francis Joseph that the death of this old embodiment of the Empire was felt by the broad masses to be tantamount to the death of the Empire itself. Indeed, it was one of the craftiest artifices, particularly of the Slavic policy, to create the appearance that the Austrian state no longer owed its existence to anything but the miraculous and unique skill of this monarch; this flattery was all the more welcome in the Hofburg, since it corresponded not at all to the real merits of the Emperor. The thorn hidden in these paeans of praise remained undiscovered. The rulers did not see, or perhaps no longer wanted to see, that the more the monarchy depended on the outstanding statecraft, as they put it, of this "wisest monarch" of all times, the more catastrophic the situation was bound to become if one day Fate were to knock at his door, too, demanding its tribute.

Was old Austria even conceivable without the Emperor?!

Wouldn't the tragedy which had once stricken Maria Theresa have been repeated?

No, it is really doing the Vienna circles an injustice to reproach them with rushing into a war which might otherwise have been avoided. It no longer could be avoided, but at most could have been postponed for one or two years. But this was the curse of German as well as Austrian diplomacy, that it had always striven to postpone the inevitable reckoning, until at length it was forced to strike at the most unfavorable hour. We can be convinced that a further attempt to save peace would have brought war at an even more unfavorable time.

No, those who did not want this war had to have the courage to face the consequences, which could have consisted only in the sacrifice of Austria. Even then the war would have come, but no longer as a struggle of all against ourselves, but in the form of a partition of the Habsburg monarchy. And then they had to make up their minds to join in, or to look on with empty hands and let Fate run its course.

Those very people, however, who today are loudest in cursing the beginning of the war and offer the sagest opinions were those who contributed most fatally to steering us into it.

For decades the Social Democrats had carried on the most scoundrelly war agitation against Russia, and the Center for religious reasons had been most active in making the Austrian state the hinge and pivot of German policy. Now we had to suffer the consequences of this lunacy. What came had to come, and could no longer under any circumstances be avoided. The guilt of the German government was that in order to preserve peace it always missed the favorable hours for striking, became entangled in the alliance for the preservation of world peace, and thus finally became the victim of a world coalition which countered the idea of preserving world peace with nothing less than determination for world war.

If the Vienna government had given the ultimatum another, milder form, this would have changed nothing in the situation except at most one thing, that this government would itself have been swept away by the indignation of the people. For in the eyes of the broad masses the tone of the ultimatum was far too gentle and by no means too brutal, let alone too far-reaching. Anyone who today attempts to argue this away is either a forgetful blockhead or a perfectly conscious swindler and liar.

The struggle of the year 1914 was not forced on the masses—no, by the living God—it was desired by the whole people.

People wanted at length to put an end to the general uncertainty. Only thus can it be understood that more than two million German men and boys thronged to the colors for this hardest of all struggles, prepared to defend the flag with the last drop of their blood.

Erich Brandenburg

A GERMAN ACADEMIC REBUTTAL

In the 1920s the German government mounted a massive campaign to discredit the Versailles "verdict" on war guilt. A major feature of that effort was the utilization of leading German historians, scholars, and publicists in the debate. One who participated was Erich Brandenburg, professor of history at the University of Leipzig and a respected expert on the process of German unification after 1848. Granted access to the

From pp. 518-523 in *From Bismarck to the World War* by Erich Brandenburg, trans. Annie E. Adams and published by Oxford University Press (1927). Reprinted by permission of the publisher.

German diplomatic archives, Brandenburg wrote a mild revisionist account of German foreign policy that blamed Russia and France for the war. But he also sought to shift the debate from the immediate July crisis to an analysis of the more fundamental issues that characterized German and European diplomacy after 1890. Further, he also posed the same question to the Triple Entente powers that had been asked of Germany in 1919: What had London, Paris, and St. Petersburg done to preserve the peace?

T HE CRIME of Sarajevo brought out the Vienna plan for a final reckoning with Serbia. It was thought that the only way to save the threatened existence of the Monarchy was to give proof to the world of its vitality by administering an exemplary chastisement of this dangerous neighbour. We [Germany] thought that we ought not to hold Austria back, and we hoped by the old methods to prevent Russia from intervening. We underestimated the dangers of that policy, and were ourselves obsessed by the feeling that if the great reckoning must come it was perhaps as well it should come now and for this cause. So we landed ourselves in a plight from which, after our vain efforts at the last moment to extricate Austria, there was no longer any outlet but war.

German policy during these years has earned many and heavy reproaches. It can justly be accused of short-sightedness, lack of method, want of forethought and of understanding of the psychology of other peoples; we can blame Germany's vacillation and her sudden recklessness, as in the Morocco question, for instance. But no one can maintain with any show of reason that at any given time she either wished for war or strove to bring it about. Had Germany really wanted war, no more favourable time could have been found than during the Russo-Japanese War. Russia was then incapable of action, France and England inadequately equipped, and the Entente only recently founded. Had we wanted a preventive war all the chances were in our favour then and up till 1909. The General Staff, as in duty bound, had called attention to that fact. But this possibility was never seriously entertained by our

Government, and even in 1909, when Austria was considering an invasion of Serbia, it worked consistently for peace. Perhaps it would have been wiser to attack boldly then, but that was not done because of the desire not to break the peace unless compelled. In spite of all the sounding words that have been spoken, our policy was, in fact, too anxious and too peace-loving rather than too militant. We never wanted to win at the expense of others, but only and always to share with them and alongside of them in the apportioning of the earth.

Can as much be said of the other Powers concerned?

As regards England, so far as we can learn from the sources at present available, no one in England really wanted war. The view so widely held in Germany that Britain engineered the war in order to destroy our economic competition, which was becoming increasingly dangerous to her, has little justification. But across the Channel they did fear our growing political and military power; they felt their own supremacy and security threatened by the growth of our battle fleet, and they credited us with the intention of seizing the hegemony of the Continent of Europe. In order to secure themselves against such possibilities and to prevent us from occupying permanently the position of arbiter, the Entente was founded when the alliance with Germany failed. English statesmen intended it to be a means of maintaining the balance of power and of keeping Germany's might and ambition within due bounds; there is no indication that it was originally intended as an instrument of war. Undoubtedly in London at the outset they underestimated the danger of dividing Europe into two hostile leagues. When they did realize it, they sought to get into touch again with Germany without surrendering the Entente, and so in a manner to recover their supremacy over the parties. But they were by that time too closely bound to the one group, and they had not the power to direct the policy of their allies entirely in the path which they desired. As they were convinced that in a war in which England took no part Germany would be victorious and become master of Europe, they were forced, if the war could not be prevented, to take sides with France and Russia; otherwise they would be faced by the very situation to escape which the Entente had been founded. So it was that England too was ultimately dependent on the decision of her allies, without wishing it, and without clearly realizing it. The fact that Grey himself felt bound to the Entente policy was naturally of great significance. But at the critical moment he might have been turned out of office. England's decisions did not depend on him alone; they were dictated by the consequences of her previous policy and by the fear of an increase of Germany's power. . . .

With France and Russia the case was quite different. I do not doubt that the great body of the people even in these two countries was desirous of peace. In the ruling circles, both in Paris and St. Petersburg, there were two parties; the one wanted peace if it could be maintained consistently with honour, the other wanted war. In France the latter combined with those who cherished the idea of *revanche,* which had never died out. Poincaré and Delcassé were its great protagonists. Since the brush with Germany in Morocco and the founding of the Entente, this party had greatly strengthened its influence; and finally, with Poincaré as leader it had assumed the real management of affairs. In Russia the Czar was the head of the peace party; for a long time the war party was without any real leader. Wide military circles and all those who favoured Pan-Slav ideas supported the war party at St. Petersburg. In Iswolski, after his personal reverse in the Bosnian crisis, they found a zealous champion. As Ambassador in Paris, this vain and vengeful man fell wholly under the sway of the Delcassé and Poincaré group and rendered it the greatest service by his personal influence. His dispatches from Paris, the publication of which in a German translation has now been completed, show clearly to anyone who is not blinded by prejudice, by what cautious and subtle methods Iswolski, in conjunction with Poincaré, prepared for the war. He knew how to get rid of refractory elements like Georges Louis, the French Ambassador in St. Petersburg, how to bribe the press and make use of it, and how to exploit the insatiable vanity of Poincaré. It is really difficult to say which of the two led and which followed. There is no doubt as to their close cooperation. Iswolski cannot repeat too often what good luck it is that Poincaré, and not some other less reliable and less skillful politician, stands at the head of France.

So far as guilt can be brought home to individual personalities in the World War, these two men stand convicted. For long years they had prepared the soil by persistent and deliberate effort, always careful not to let their real aims appear, but to wait for the time when the armaments were completed and when one of the opposing Powers, through some indiscretion, offered the possibility of being made to appear the aggressor; for that was necessary not only to win over the opinion of the masses in both countries, but also out of consideration for England, with her cautious Government and peace-loving people. But the aims which these groups pursued could not be achieved without war. The French wished to recover Alsace-Lorraine from the Germans; the Russians wished to open the way to the Straits and to the control of the Balkans, and they wished to free the Slavs from the German, Austrian, and Turkish domination under which they had hitherto lived, and to absorb them within their own sphere of influence. It was they, not Germany, who wished for conquests at the expense of others.

The clever and unscrupulous tunneling operations of these comparatively small groups prepared the way for the World War.

Their leaders were not daunted by the hideous consequences of such a struggle of the nations, for without it they could not reach their goal. They were already waiting their opportunity during the Balkan Wars, and in July 1914 they seized it gladly. The Russian mobilization, which was the immediate cause of the war, was their work.

Unfortunately we possessed no statesman who was competent to deal with these clever and unscrupulous diplomatists. Austria's rashness and Germany's timid consideration for her last ally gave them the opportunity which they wanted, and they used it with consummate skill.

I have purposely confined myself in all these considerations to the interrelation of the immediate causes of the war, but I cannot close the book without referring briefly to the deeper reasons for this great catastrophe.

The rapid partitioning of Africa and of the South Sea Islands among the European Powers, from about 1880 onwards, created an atmosphere of acute political tension. This was further accentuated after 1895, when it seemed as if the process of dismemberment were to be applied in the Far East and to the territory of Turkey. So long as there was land to dispose of, a policy of compensations served as a safety valve and prevented explosions. But the narrower the available space became, the more stiffly the valve worked and the more it creaked. America's intervention in the Far East and Japan's accession to the dignity of a Great Power, practically closed the whole of eastern Asia against dismemberment for a long time to come. After 1900 the territory of Africa had all been allotted as far as Morocco and Abyssinia. The competition among the Powers was now concentrated on Morocco and the Turkish Empire.

Underlying these international and colonial rivalries lay the powerful economic interests of the leading industrial and commercial nations, each of them anxious to get as large a field as possible for the sale of its goods, and to secure productive sources for the supply of raw materials, and political privileges to ensure remunerative investment for its capital.

Alongside these new international antagonisms there remained the old enmities between the Continental Powers. The greatest of these was the Franco-German rivalry symbolized in Alsace-Lorraine, and the struggle between Austria-Hungary and Russia for the leading position in the Balkans.

Yet underneath these European antagonisms there lay a deeper difficulty. It was the discord which increased throughout the nineteenth century between the State frontiers as settled of old, or as established by treaty, and the principle of nationality, established with such conquering power by the French Revolution. Neither in Eastern Europe, nor in the Balkans, nor between France and Germany, did the boundaries of the States correspond with those of population and language. Austria-Hungary and Turkey were States belonging to an earlier stage of development. They had been created without any regard to the nationality and the wish of the human beings composing them, and they were only maintained with difficulty by the pressure of circumstances. Germany, too, in the northeast, was ruling a large foreign population, and, in 1871, she had absorbed within her empire a French-speaking territory, even if according to its character and to the majority of its inhabitants, it was a national entity in itself.

If the principle of nationality remained the foundation of European States—during these last decades it had grown greatly in strength and significance—these anachronistic States belonging to an earlier generation had to be broken up and removed. Nothing could save them from this fate. When Germany, not realizing this position, bound up her destiny with that of Austria-Hungary and for a long time supported the effort to maintain and strengthen the Turkish Empire, she committed a gross and disastrous mistake from the point of view of historical development. She linked up her fresh and vigorous national strength with the corrupt remnant of a decaying empire doomed to destruction, and was thereby involved in its ruin. The maintenance of the

Danube Monarchy, as a barrier against the flooding of southeastern Europe by Slav races under Russian leadership, was certainly part of the traditions of the Bismarck School; yet how often Bismarck himself warned us against letting ourselves be pushed into the flames for the expansion of Austria's interests in the Balkans! And that is precisely what happened. . . .By exalting into an inviolable dogma the necessity for the Triple Alliance and for the maintenance of the Danube Monarchy, our statesmen were acting contrary to the spirit of Bismarck and of all sound policy, and robbed themselves of the freedom of movement indispensable for the development of our system of alliances.

Harry E. Barnes

FRANCE AND RUSSIA ACCUSED: THE EXTREME REVISIONIST CASE

No revisionist writer in any country exceeded Harry E. Barnes in his systematic denunciation of the Versailles accusations against the Central Powers. And few writers so cogently and polemically framed a counter-set of indictments against France and Russia. Barnes came to epitomize for many the "revisionist" view of the origins of the war and to render suspect other, more dispassionate accounts.

A young professor of sociology and history at Smith College in the early 1920s, Barnes, like many Americans, found the "orthodox" accusations heavy-handed, biased, and one-sided. Impulsively and often with great imagination Barnes culled the welter of rapidly appearing diplomatic documents to produce in 1926 the volume from which this selection is taken. Not surprisingly the German Foreign Office would later bestow copies of the book on many libraries and historical institutes. In many respects Article 231 and Barnes's arguments represent the most extreme statements on the origins of the World War. Writers and historians have since generally fallen between the two positions, though some have nearly been at one extreme or the other.

WE HAVE now devoted a series of chapters to the question of war responsibility in each of the major states involved. We may here briefly summarize the general situation in what may be regarded as a brief statement of the revisionist point of view as it appears to the present writer. The general European system after 1870, based as it was upon nationalism, militarism, secret alliances, and imperialistic aims, naturally inclined Europe toward war. The system does not, however, explain why war came in 1914, as the same general European situation had been prevailing for many years prior to that time, though certain problems had become more acute in the years immediately preceding the World War, particularly in the Near East and Morocco.

The Franco-Russian Alliance concluded by 1894 was transformed into an offensive organization following 1912 through the cooperation of Izvolski and Poincaré. Both recognized that the chief objects of Russian and French foreign policy, the seizure of the Straits and the return of Alsace-Lorraine, could be realized only through a general European war. From 1912-1914 their joint plans involved a manipulation of the Balkan situation in such a fashion as to be able to take advantage of any crisis likely to provoke a European war, an arrangement to get England so involved that she would be bound to come in on the side of France and Russia, and a great increase in military preparations in France and Russia.

It was decided that Serbia would be the most favorable area in which to create the desired incident in the Balkans. In the early spring of 1914 prominent officers in the Serbian General Staff laid a plot for the assassination of the Archduke, Franz Ferdinand. The Serbian civil government was aware of the plot for at least a month before its execution, but made no adequate effort to stop the plot or to warn Austria. Prominent Russians were also aware of the plot, but the degree of the complicity of Russia is as yet uncertain.

When the assassination came, the French and Russians recognized that the impending clash between Austria and Serbia would constitute a highly appropriate episode over which to bring about the desired conflict. The year 1914 was a particularly desirable year for the Entente because there was imminent danger that England might develop more happy relations with Germany, and that the French Radicals might be able to secure the repeal of the French Army Bill. Poincaré went to St. Petersburg and, before knowing the terms of the Austrian ultimatum, renewed his pledge of two years earlier to support Russia in a war over the Balkans, and indicated that the probable Austro-Serbian conflict would meet the conditions demanded by the French in supporting Russia in intervention in the Balkans.

The Franco-Russian procedure in 1914 was to indicate a show of conciliation and concessions on the part of Serbia, and apparent Franco-Russian willingness to settle the dispute through diplomacy, while secret Franco-Russian military preparations were to be carried on which would ultimately make a diplomatic settlement quite impossible. Hence, Russia urged Serbia not to declare war on Austria and, to insure a sufficiently conciliatory Serbian reply to Austria, the Serbian response to the Austrian ultimatum was drafted in outline in the French Foreign Office. Russia did not desire to have Serbia precipitate matters prematurely by a declaration of war on Austria, because this would have affected European opinion, particularly English opinion, unfavorably and would also have brought about military activities altogether too rapidly for Russia, whose mobilization over a vast area would necessarily be slow as compared with that of Austria and Germany.

On the 24th of July, the moment Russia and France learned of the terms of the Austrian ultimatum to Serbia, they began that dual program of diplomatic barrage combined with secret military preparations which had made a European war inevitable by the afternoon of July 30th. Russia sent a diplomatic message to Serbia counseling moderation, but at the same time decided upon the mobilization of the four great military districts of Central and Southern Russia as well as of the Russian fleets. Russian money in Germany and Austria was also called in.

On the same day Viviani telegraphed to the French Foreign Office that the Austro-Serbian situation was likely to develop serious European complications, and the French troops in Morocco were ordered home. Both countries began systematic military preparations for war on the 26th of July. By the 29th the time had come when Russian military preparations had gone far enough to warrant a general mobilization, and the Tsar was persuaded to consent to this order. A telegram from the Kaiser, however, induced him to revoke the order, but the next day Sazonov and the army officials once more extracted from the Tsar his reluctant consent to the order for general mobilization. The French and the Russians had understood for a generation that once Russian general mobilization was ordered there would be no way of preventing a general European war. General Dobrorolski has told us with great candor that the Russian authorities in 1914 fully realized that a European war was *on* as soon as the mobilization order had been sent out of the general telegraph office in St. Petersburg late in the afternoon of July 30th.

The French authorities had been thoroughly informed as to the nature and progress of the Russian military preparations, but they made no effort to restrain them, though the French well knew that these military activities were bound to render a European war inevitable. They actually urged the Russians to speed up their military preparations, but to be more secretive about them, so as not to alienate England or provoke Germany to counter-mobilization. On the night of July 31st the French government went still further and finally decided for war, handing this information to Izvolski about midnight of the 31st. France was, thus, the first country to declare itself for war in the European crisis of 1914.

The Austrian statesmen in 1914 decided that the time had come when it would be necessary to control the Serbian menace, and they consciously planned an ultimatum to Serbia of such severity that it would be practically impossible for Serbia to concede all of these demands. The plan, then, was to make a show of diplomacy but to move toward certain war. This program was much like that of France and Russia, save for the fact that *Austria desired to provoke nothing but a local punitive war while the plans of France and Russia envisaged a general European conflict.* This is the most important point to be borne in mind when estimating the relative war guilt of Austria as against that of France and Russia.

Germany, formerly friendly to Serbia, was alarmed by the assassination of the Archduke and the resulting menace to her chief ally. Germany therefore agreed to stand behind Austria in the plan of the latter to execute her program of punishing Serbia. The answer of the Serbians to the Austrian ultimatum, however, impressed the Kaiser as satisfactory, and from that time on he was opposed to further military activity on the part of Austria against Serbia.

In cooperation with Sir Edward Grey, Germany began on the 27th of July to urge upon Austria direct negotiations with Russia and the mediation of her dispute with Serbia. Austria at first refused to listen to this advice and declared war upon Serbia on the 28th. Germany then became alarmed at the rumored Russian military preparations and vigorously pressed Austria for a diplomatic settlement of the dispute. Austria did not give way and consent to this until the 31st of July, which was too late to avert a general European war because the Russian mobilization was then in full swing. Germany endeavored without success to secure the suspension of military activities by Russia, and then, after unexpected hesitation and deliberation, declared war on Russia.

The Russian general mobilization, undertaken with the full connivance of the French, was ordered at a time when diplomatic negotiations were moving rapidly toward a satisfactory settlement of the major problems in the crisis. Hence, the Russian general mobilization not only initiated military hostilities, but was also the sole reason for the failure of diplomatic efforts.

England was for peace, provided France was not drawn into the conflict, but was determined to come into the War in case France was involved. As France decided from the beginning to stand with Russia for war, and as England refused to attempt to restrain either France or Russia, England was inevitably drawn away from her encouragement of the German efforts towards a diplomatic settlement of the crisis and into the support of the military aggression of France and Russia. She made her decision to enter the War after Germany had proposed to keep out of Belgium and to refrain from attacking France if England would remain neutral. In fact, Germany even suggested that she might guarantee the integrity of France and the French colonies in the event of war if England would promise neutrality. The Belgian issue in England was a pure subterfuge, exploited by Sir Edward Grey to inflame British opinion against Germany and to secure British support of his war policy. . . .

In estimating the order of guilt of the various countries we may safely say that the only direct and immediate responsibility for the World War falls upon Serbia, France and Russia, with the guilt about equally distributed. Next in order—far below France and Russia—would come Austria, though she never desired a general European war. Finally, we should place Germany and England as tied for last place, both being opposed to war in the 1914 crisis. Probably the German public was somewhat more favorable to military activities than the English people, but, as we have amply explained above, the Kaiser made much more strenuous efforts to preserve the peace of Europe in 1914 than did Sir Edward Grey.

Sidney B. Fay

A MODERATE REVISIONIST: MULTIPLE RESPONSIBILITY

More than fifty years have passed since the appearance of Sidney Fay's two-volume study, *The Origins of the World War.* Yet this scholarly, sober work, written before the publication of the French or Austro-Hungarian documents, remains one of the most thoughtful, balanced assessments of the outbreak of the war. Heralded first by a series of articles in the *American Historical Review* in 1920-1921 and other pieces in 1925 on Serbia's complicity in the events at Sarajevo, Fay's 1928 study demonstrated superb mastery of the rapidly appearing documentation. In it he analyzed the interaction between the long-term causes of the war (which he defined as secret alliances, militarism, nationalism, economic imperialism, and the press) and the events of July-August 1914. At every turn Fay (who had been a colleague of Barnes at Smith before going to Harvard in 1929) remembered the pressures that the governments and their statesmen faced in actual decision making. He did not forget that policymakers get tired, make mistakes, have wistful thoughts, and are often less than diabolical. Because of their fairness his moderate revisionist views have enjoyed (and continue to enjoy) widespread acceptance among those who find the assertions of Article 231 too simplistic and dogmatic. Sidney Fay lifted the discussion of war causation above the polemical and toward a more scholarly, careful examination of the evidence. His two volumes remain a monument to American historical scholarship.

Reprinted with permission of Macmillan Publishing Co., Inc. from *The Origins of the World War* by Sidney B. Fay, 2nd edition, pp. 547-558. Copyright 1928, 1930 by Macmillan Publishing Co., Inc.; renewed 1956, 1958 by Sidney Bradshaw Fay.

NONE OF THE Powers wanted a European War. Their governing rulers and ministers, with very few exceptions, all foresaw that it must be a frightful struggle, in which the political results were not absolutely certain, but in which the loss of life, suffering, and economic consequences were bound to be terrible. This is true, in a greater or less degree, of Pashitch, Berchtold, Bethmann, Sazonoff, Poincaré, San Giuliano and Sir Edward Grey. Yet none of them, not even Sir Edward Grey, could have foreseen that the political results were to be so stupendous, and the other consequences so terrible, as was actually the case.

For many of the Powers, to be sure, a European War might seem to hold out the possibility of achieving various desired advantages: for Serbia, the achievement of national unity for all Serbs; for Austria, the revival of her waning prestige as a Great Power, and the checking of nationalistic tendencies which threatened her very existence; for Russia, the accomplishment of her historic mission of controlling Constantinople and the Straits; for Germany, new economic advantages and the restoration of the European balance which had changed with the weakening of the Triple Alliance and the tightening of the Triple Entente; for France, the recovery of Alsace-Lorraine and the ending of the German menace; and for England, the destruction of the German naval danger and of Prussian militarism. All these advantages, and many others, were feverishly striven and intrigued for, on all sides, the moment the War actually broke out, but this is no good proof that any of the statesmen mentioned deliberately aimed to bring about a war to secure these advantages. One cannot judge the motives which actuated men before the War, by what they did in an absolutely new situation which arose as soon as they were overtaken by a conflagration they had sought to avert. And in fact, in the case of the two Powers between whom the immediate conflict arose, the postponement or avoidance of a European War would have facilitated the accomplishment of the ultimate advantages aimed at: Pashitch knew that there was a better chance for Serbian national unity after he had consolidated Serbian gains in the Balkan Wars, and after Russia had completed her military and naval armaments as planned for 1917; and Berchtold knew that he had a better chance of crushing the Greater Serbia danger and strengthening Austria, if he could avoid Russian intervention and a general European War. . . .

Nevertheless, a European War broke out. Why? Because in each country political and military leaders did certain things which led to mobilizations and declarations of war, or failed to do certain things which might have prevented them. In this sense, all the European countries, in a greater or less degree, were responsible. One must abandon the dictum of the Versailles Treaty that Germany and her allies were solely responsible. It was a dictum exacted by victors from vanquished, under the influence of the blindness, ignorance, hatred, and the propagandist misconceptions to which war had given rise. It was based on evidence which was incomplete and not always sound. It is generally recognized by the best historical scholars in all countries to be no longer tenable or defensible. They are agreed that the responsibility for the War is a divided responsibility. But they still disagree very much as to the relative part of this responsibility that falls on each country and on each individual political or military leader.

Some writers like to fix positively in some precise mathematical fashion the exact responsibility for the War. This was done in one way by the framers of Article 231 of the Treaty of Versailles. It has been done in other ways by those who would fix the responsibility in some relative fashion, as, for instance, Austria first, then Russia, France and Germany and England. But the present writer deprecates such efforts to assess by a precise formula a very complicated question, which is after all more a matter of delicate shading than of definite white and black. Oversimplification, as Napoleon once said in framing his Code, is the enemy of precision. Moreover, even supposing that a general consensus of opinion might be reached as to the relative responsibility of any individual country or man for immediate causes connected with the July crisis of 1914, it is by no means necessarily true that the same relative responsibility would hold for the underlying causes, which for years had been tending toward the creation of a dangerous situation.

One may, however, sum up very briefly the most salient facts in regard to each country.

Serbia felt a natural and justifiable impulse to do what so many other countries had done in the nineteenth century—to bring under one national Government all the discontented Serb people. She had liberated those under Turkish rule; the next step was to liberate those under Hapsburg rule. She looked to Russia for assistance, and had been encouraged to expect that she would receive it. After the assassination, Mr. Pashitch took no steps to discover and bring to justice Serbians in Belgrade who had been implicated in the plot. One of them, Ciganovitch, was even assisted to disappear. Mr. Pashitch waited to see what evidence the Austrian authorities could find. When Austria demanded cooperation of Austrian officials in discovering, though not in trying, implicated Serbians, the Serbian Government made a very conciliatory but negative reply. They expected that the reply would not be regarded as satisfactory, and, even before it was given, ordered the mobilization of the Serbian army. Serbia did not want war, but believed it would be forced upon her. That Mr. Pashitch was aware of the plot three weeks before it was executed, failed to take effective steps to prevent the assassins from crossing over from Serbia to Bosnia, and then failed to give Austria any warning or information which might have averted the fatal crime, were facts unknown to Austria in July, 1914; they cannot therefore be regarded as in any way justifying Austria's conduct; but they are part of Serbia's responsibility, and a very serious part.

Austria was more responsible for the immediate origin of the war than any other Power. Yet from her own point of view she was acting in self-defense—not against an immediate military attack, but against the cor-

roding Greater Serbia and Jugoslav agitation which her leaders believed threatened her very existence. No State can be expected to sit with folded arms and await dismemberment at the hands of its neighbors. Russia was believed to be intriguing with Serbia and Rumania against the Dual Monarchy. The assassination of the heir to the throne, as a result of a plot prepared in Belgrade, demanded severe retribution; otherwise Austria would be regarded as incapable of action, "worm-eaten" as the Serbian press expressed it, would sink in prestige, and hasten her own downfall. To avert this Berthtold determined to crush Serbia with war. He deliberately framed the ultimatum with the expectation and hope that it would be rejected. He hurriedly declared war against Serbia in order to forestall all efforts at mediation. He refused even to answer his own ally's urgent requests to come to an understanding with Russia, on the basis of a military occupation of Belgrade as a pledge that Serbia would carry out the promises in her reply to the ultimatum. Berchtold gambled on a "local" war with Serbia only, believing that he could rattle the German sword; but rather than abandon his war with Serbia, he was ready to drag the rest of Europe into war.

It is very questionable whether Berchtold's obstinate determination to diminish Serbia and destroy her as a Balkan factor was, after all, the right method, even if he had succeeded in keeping the war "localized" and in temporarily strengthening the Dual Monarchy. Supposing that Russia in 1914, because of military unpreparedness or lack of support, had been ready to tolerate the execution of Berchtold's designs, it is quite certain that she would have aimed within the next two or three years at wiping out this second humiliation, which was so much more damaging to her prestige than that of 1908-1909. In two or three years, when her great program of military reform was finally completed, Russia would certainly have found a pretext to reverse the balance in the Balkans in her own favor again. A further consequence of Berchtold's policy, even if successful, would have been the still closer consolidation of the Triple

Entente, with the possible addition of Italy. And, finally, a partially dismembered Serbia would have become a still greater source of unrest and danger to the peace of Europe than heretofore. Serbian nationalism, like Polish nationalism, would have been intensified by partition. Austrian power and prestige would not have been so greatly increased as to be able to meet these new dangers. Berchtold's plan was a mere temporary improvement, but could not be a final solution of the Austro-Serbian antagonism. Franz Ferdinand and many others recognized this, and so long as he lived, no step in this fatal direction had been taken. It was the tragic fate of Austria that the only man who might have had the power and ability to develop Austria along sound lines became the innocent victim of the crime which was the occasion of the World War and so of her ultimate disruption.

Germany did not plot a European War, did not want one, and made genuine, though too belated efforts, to avert one. She was the victim of her alliance with Austria and of her own folly. Austria was her only dependable ally, Italy and Rumania having become nothing but allies in name. She could not throw her over, as otherwise she would stand isolated between Russia, where Pan-Slavism and armaments were growing stronger every year, and France, where Alsace-Lorraine, Delcassé's fall, and Agadir were not forgotten. Therefore, Bethmann felt bound to accede to Berchtold's request for support and gave him a free hand to deal with Serbia; he also hoped and expected to "localize" the Austro-Serbian conflict. Germany then gave grounds to the Entente for suspecting the sincerity of her peaceful intentions by her denial of any foreknowledge of the ultimatum, by her support and justification of it when it was published, and by her refusal of Sir Edward Grey's conference proposal. However, Germany by no means had Austria so completely under her thumb as the Entente Powers and many writers have assumed. It is true that Berchtold would hardly have embarked on his gambler's policy unless he had been assured that Germany would fulfill the obligations of the

alliance, and to this extent Germany must share the great responsibility of Austria. But when Bethmann realized that Russia was likely to intervene, that England might not remain neutral, and that there was danger of a world war of which Germany and Austria would appear to be the instigators, he tried to call a halt on Austria, but it was too late. He pressed mediation proposals on Vienna, but Berchtold was insensible to the pressure, and the Entente Powers did not believe in the sincerity of his pressure, especially as they produced no results.

Germany's geographical position between France and Russia, and her inferiority in number of troops, had made necessary the plan of crushing the French army quickly at first and then turning against Russia. This was only possible, in the opinion of her strategists, by marching through Belgium, as it was generally anticipated by military men that she would do in case of a European War. On July 29, after Austria had declared war on Serbia, and after the Tsar had asserted to general mobilization in Russia (though this was not known in Berlin and was later postponed for a day owing to the Kaiser's telegram to the Tsar), Bethmann took the precaution of sending to the German Minister in Brussels a sealed envelope. The Minister was not to open it except on further instructions. It contained the later demand for the passage of the German army through Belgium. This does not mean, however, that Germany had decided for war. In fact, Bethmann was one of the last of the statesmen to abandon hope of peace and to consent to the mobilization of his country's army. General mobilization of the continental armies took place in the following order: Serbia, Russia, Austria, France and Germany. General mobilization by a Great Power was commonly interpreted by military men in every country, though perhaps not by Sir Edward Grey, the Tsar, and some civilian officials, as meaning that the country was on the point of making war—that the military machine had begun to move and would not be stopped. Hence, when Germany learned of the Russian general mobilization, she sent ultimatums to St.

Petersburg and Paris, warning that German mobilization would follow unless Russia suspended hers within twelve hours, and asking what would be the attitude of France. The answers being unsatisfactory, Germany then mobilized and declared war. It was the hasty Russian general mobilization, assented to on July 29 and ordered on July 30, while Germany was still trying to bring Austria to accept mediation proposals, which finally rendered the European War inevitable.

Russia was partly responsible for the Austro-Serbian conflict because of the frequent encouragement which she had given at Belgrade—that Serbian national unity would be ultimately achieved with Russian assistance at Austrian expense. This had led the Belgrade Cabinet to hope for Russian support in case of a war with Austria, and the hope did not prove vain in July, 1914. Before this, to be sure, in the Bosnian Crisis and during the Balkan Wars, Russia had put restraint upon Serbia, because Russia, exhausted by the effects of Russo-Japanese War, was not yet ready for a European struggle with the Teutonic Powers. But in 1914 her armaments, though not yet completed, had made such progress that the militarists were confident of success, if they had French and British support. In the spring of 1914 the Minister of War, Sukhomlinov, had published an article in a Russian newspaper, though without signing his name, to the effect, "Russia is ready, France must be ready also." Austria was convinced that Russia would ultimately aid Serbia, unless the Serbian danger were dealt with energetically after the Archduke's murder; she knew that Russia was growing stronger every year; but she doubted whether the Tsar's armaments had yet reached the point at which Russia would dare to intervene; she would therefore run less risk of Russian intervention and a European War if she used the Archduke's assassination as an excuse for weakening Serbia, than if she should postpone action until the future.

Russia's responsibility lay also in the secret preparatory military measures which she was making at the same time that she was carrying on diplomatic negotiations.

These alarmed Germany and Austria. But it was primarily Russia's general mobilization, made when Germany was trying to bring Austria to a settlement, which precipitated the final catastrophe, causing Germany to mobilize and declare war.

The part of France is less clear than that of the other Great Powers because she has not yet made a full publication of her documents. To be sure, M. Poincaré, in the fourth volume of his memoirs, has made a skillful and elaborate plea to prove *La France innocente*. But he is not convincing. It is quite clear that on his visit to Russia he assured the Tsar's government that France would support her as an ally in preventing Austria from humiliating or crushing Serbia. Paléologue renewed these assurances in a way to encourage Russia to take a strong hand. He did not attempt to restrain Russia from military measures which he knew would call forth German countermeasures and cause war. Nor did he keep his government promptly and fully informed of the military steps which were being taken at St. Petersburg. President Poincaré, upon his return to France, made efforts for peace, but his great preoccupation was to minimize French and Russian preparatory measures and emphasize those of Germany, in order to secure the certainty of British support in a struggle which he now regarded as inevitable.

Sir Edward Grey made many sincere proposals for preserving peace; they all failed owing partly, but not exclusively, to Germany's attitude. Sir Edward could probably have prevented war if he had done either of two things. If, early in the crisis, he had acceded to the urging of France and Russia and given a strong warning to Germany that, in a European war, England would take the side of the Franco-Russian Alliance, this would probably have led Bethmann to exert an earlier and more effective pressure on Austria; and it would perhaps thereby have prevented the Austrian declaration of war on Serbia and brought to a successful issue the "direct conversations" between Vienna and St. Petersburg. Or, if Sir Edward Grey had listened to German urging and warned

France and Russia early in the crisis that if they became involved in war, England would remain neutral, probably Russia would have hesitated with her mobilizations, and France would probably have exerted a restraining influence at St. Petersburg. But Sir Edward Grey could not say that England would take the side of France and Russia because he had a Cabinet nearly evenly divided, and he was not sure, early in the crisis, that public opinion in England would back him up in war against Germany. He could resign, and he says in his memoirs that he would have resigned but that would have been no comfort or aid to France, who had come confidently to count upon British support. He was determined to say and do nothing which might encourage her with a hope which he could not fulfill. Therefore, in spite of the pleadings of the French, he refused to give them definite assurances until the probable German determination to go through Belgium made it clear that the Cabinet, and Parliament, and British public opinion would follow his lead in war on Germany. On the other hand, he was unwilling to heed the German pleadings that he exercise restraint at Paris and St. Petersburg, because he did not wish to endanger the Anglo-Russian Entente and the solidarity of the Triple Entente, because he felt a moral obligation to France, growing out of the Anglo-French military and naval conversations of the past years, and because he suspected that Germany was backing Austria up in an unjustifiable course and that Prussian militarists had taken the direction of affairs in Berlin out of the hands of Herr von Bethmann-Hollweg and the civilian authorities.

Italy exerted relatively little influence on the crisis in either direction.

Belgium had done nothing in any way to justify the demand which Germany made upon her. With commendable prudence, at the very first news of the ominous Austrian ultimatum, she had foreseen the danger to which she might be exposed. She had accordingly instructed her representatives abroad as to the statements which they were to make in case Belgium should decide very

suddenly to mobilize to protect her neutrality. On July 29 she placed her army upon "a strengthened war footing," but did not order complete mobilization until two days later, when Austria, Russia, and Germany had already done so, and war appeared inevitable. Even after being confronted with the terrible German ultimatum at 7 p.m. on August 2, she did not at once invite the assistance of English and French troops to aid her in the defense of her soil and her neutrality against a certain German assault; it was not until German troops had actually violated her territory on August 4 that she appealed for the assistance of the Powers which had guaranteed her neutrality. Belgium was the innocent victim of German strategic necessity. Though the German violation of Belgium was of enormous influence in forming public opinion as to the responsibility for the war after hostilities began, it was not a cause of the War, except insofar as it made it easier for Sir Edward Grey to bring England into it.

In the forty years following the Franco-Prussian War, as we have seen, there developed a system of alliances which divided Europe into two hostile groups. This hostility was accentuated by the increase of armaments, economic rivalry, nationalist ambitions and antagonisms, and newspaper incitement. But it is very doubtful whether all these dangerous tendencies would have actually led to war, had it not been for the assassination of Franz Ferdinand. That was the factor which consolidated the elements of hostility and started the rapid and complicated succession of events which culminated in a World War, and for that factor Serbian nationalism was primarily responsible.

But the verdict of the Versailles Treaty that Germany and her allies were responsible for the War, in view of the evidence now available, is historically unsound. It should therefore be revised. However, because of the popular feeling widespread in some of the Entente countries, it is doubtful whether a formal and legal revision is as yet practicable. There must first come a further revision by historical scholars, and through them of public opinion.

Luigi Albertini

GERMAN RESPONSIBILITY REAFFIRMED:
A SUMMARY

The most exhaustive, thorough study of the July crisis remains Luigi Albertini's *Le origini della guerra del 1914*, first published in 1942 and translated into English in the 1950s. A former Italian senator and editor of the famous Milan newspaper, *Corriere della Sera*, Albertini was a major Italian political and press figure in the years before World War I. Later, when harassed by Mussolini, he turned his considerable talent, extraordinary contacts, and indefatigable energy to writing and compiling the three-volume study. In his efforts Albertini interviewed many of the decision makers of 1914, corresponded with others, and was the first scholar-student to utilize all the diplomatic documents published by the respective governments. What emerged was in part history, in part documentary compilation, and in part wise commentary on the foibles of men and the states in which they live. Employing a diplomatic and strategic approach, his work possibly represents the quintessential practice of diplomatic history.

In the years since its publication (and especially since its translation by Isabella Massey), Albertini's contribution has become an indispensable guide to any study of the long- and the short-range causes of the war. Its fairness and thoroughness unquestioned, Albertini's major contention—that Germany was principally responsible and Austria-Hungary secondarily so for the war—reaffirmed the more orthodox views of the victorious powers. Its presence, moreover, has influenced all subsequent writing on the topic: indeed, many later historians, seeking novelty, often find that Albertini has in fact already made their point or certainly suggested or implied it. This is true of the German school of Fritz Fischer as well as of others. Many of Albertini's ideas have seen expression in recent surveys of the period before the World War such as Dwight Lee's *Europe's Crucial Years: The Diplomatic Background of World War I, 1902-1914*; L. F. C. Turner's *Origins of the First World War*; Oron J. Hale's *The Great Illusion, 1900-1914*; Laurence Lafore's *The Long Fuse*; and Joachim Remak's *The Origins of World War I, 1871-1914*.

Yet because Albertini died before he could write a concluding chapter such as those by Fay and Barnes, his ideas have not—despite their influence—been represented in a book of readings. In an attempt to overcome this omission, the editor has prepared the following summary of some of Albertini's many assessments, emphasizing his interpretations and major factual contributions to the study of the outbreak of the war.

Summary based on Luigi Albertini, *Le origini della guerra del 1914* (3 vols., Milan, 1942-1943), trans. Isabella Massey, *The Origins of the War of 1914* (3 vols., London, 1952-1957).

ALBERTINI, like Sidney Fay, devoted an entire volume to the background and long-range causes of the war. In doing so he did not imply that the war was inevitable (indeed, he believed it could have been avoided even after Sarajevo), only that no understanding of the decisions taken in 1914 could be divorced from the events that preceded them. The development, renewal, and enlargement of the alliance and entente structures were commented upon in great detail, especially Italy's role in them. The political problems of the Habsburg monarchy received close scrutiny: its ambitions in Bosnia-Herzegovina, its frustrations with Italy, its difficulties with the Slav groups within and without its borders. Once the Balkan wars began in 1912, Albertini believed that Vienna had only two options vis-à-vis Serbia: conciliation or destruction. And he argued that any understanding of Vienna's decision in 1914 must be placed in the context of its frustrations with Serbia from 1912 to 1914. At the same time he repeatedly stressed that Habsburg policy-makers lacked the will to act decisively. Albertini was also critical of Russia for its part in creating the Balkan League in 1912. Further, he believed that French President Raymond Poincaré and Russian Foreign Minister Sazonov were both responsible for injecting a more nationalistic, ambitious tone into the Franco-Russian alliance after 1912.

In his study of the longer-term causes Albertini did not, aside from the description of the alliance, examine the German position in and of itself. The Anglo-German naval race was scarcely mentioned, and the two Moroccan crises received nods but not much more. Still, he left no doubt of the central position occupied by Germany in European diplomacy or of the fact that eyes always turned first to Berlin. Finally, his analysis of the background of the war closed with a set of reminders about the most pressing diplomatic and strategic issues as they appeared in June of the summer of 1914: Russo-German relations embittered by the Liman von Sanders affair and the recent press exchanges; Italy and Austria-Hungary at odds

over the future of Albania; Russia successfully wooing Rumania away from the Triple Alliance; the military and naval preparations of the Triple Alliance and the Triple Entente recently reviewed and expanded.

Also, like Fay, Albertini devoted copious attention to the part played by Serbia in the assassinations. This was done less to show that Serbia caused the war than to show—as had Fay—the multiple threads of explanation and responsibility involved in the 1914 crisis. His account of the conspiracy reflected a wide correspondence, interviews with many of the survivors, and a careful attention to the material released (or suppressed) by the Yugoslav government during the interwar years. From these efforts he concluded: that Colonel Dimitrievic ("Apis") had the key role in the plot; that the senior civilian officials of the government were aware of the plot; that Belgrade made a weak attempt to alert Vienna; that Vienna mistakenly accused the Narodna Odbrana, and not the Black Hand, of the plot and thereby weakened its case. Still, Albertini asserted that it was only chance— the misdirection of Franz Ferdinand's car at the fateful corner in Sarajevo—that allowed the two shots to be fired. For all the conspiracy, it came very close to being aborted.

In his examination of the July crisis itself, Albertini reached the following conclusions which the editor has grouped together by country:

Germany: Berlin bore principal responsibility (Albertini eschewed the words "war guilt") for causing the World War. Not only did the Germans agree to Austria-Hungary's demands for support, but the government officials positively pressured Vienna to take action against Serbia. The Germans, though they did not frame the ultimatum, knew of its thrust and goals. Throughout, localization of the war, not its prevention, was Berlin's main preoccupation and would remain so until it appeared that neither Russia nor Britain would stand aside. Albertini was especially critical of Chancellor Bethmann Hollweg for failing to realize the dangers (until too late) and for having deliberately compromised the mediation efforts. The chancellor's efforts to make Russia appear the culprit drew Albertini's ire as well. He also believed that had Berlin pressed the "Halt in Belgrade" scheme more insistently, it might have offered a way out of the crisis. Finally, Albertini criticized the German military for injecting themselves into the decision process with their demands for counter measures and with the very rigidity of the Schlieffen Plan. It was the operation of these latter—military—factors that led Albertini to conclude that by August 1, 1914, everything had the atmosphere of an "epilogue of tragedy."

Austria-Hungary: If Germany was responsible for setting in motion the World War, it was Vienna that launched the local war that set the larger machine moving. Foreign Minister Berchtold was now ready for action: he seized the German assent to move his policy forward and to convince Hungarian Premier Tisza to go along. Berchtold then framed an ultimatum that could not be accepted and thereafter sought to accelerate the pace at every point: in declaring war, in ordering general mobilization, in allowing shots to be fired, and in frustrating opportunities for a diplomatic solution. In doing so, at every step Austria-Hungary revealed its determination to seek a military solution to the Serbian problem.

Russia: Albertini, like Fay (and unlike Fritz Fischer), devoted considerable attention to Russia's behavior in the crisis. There was in St. Petersburg a belligerent tone during the French state visit and this tone lingered. It was, moreover, Sazonov who talked on July 24th of partial mobilization, and it would be Russia that ordered some measures preliminary to mobilization that could easily be construed as steps toward mobilization. And it would be Sazonov on July 30th who would press for Russia's general mobilization, a step that could only escalate the crisis. (Albertini took pains to show that it was Russia, not Austria-Hungary, that first ordered general mobilization.) He also inferred that it may have been Russia's influence that prompted Serbia to be less than conciliatory in answering some

points of the Habsburg ultimatum: that is, that word from St. Petersburg stiffened Serbia's will.

Britain: Sir Edward Grey and British diplomacy did not fare well at the hands of Albertini. He blamed Grey for having entirely misunderstood the dangers of the situation in early July and for not moving decisively enough later, either to warn the Germans or to restrain the Russians and the French. He faulted Grey for letting Berlin control the timing of mediation attempts and for failing to define for Berlin the logic that would impel British intervention. Although conceding that domestic political difficulties existed for Grey, Albertini asserted that British ambivalence led both sides into serious miscalculations.

Serbia: The Belgrade government was chastised by Albertini for its failure to meet Vienna halfway: its failure to launch a convincing investigation into the plot; its strained silence on the possible involvement of the Serbian military; and its unwillingness to express more than cursory regrets over the Sarajevo murders. Albertini also believed that Belgrade would have done better to have been more compliant in responding to the ultimatum. None of this was, in his opinion, responsible behavior.

France: Albertini did not spare Paris. He found Poincaré's nationalism excessive and he was sharply critical of French unwillingness to restrain St. Petersburg in July. He did acknowledge that the absence of Poincaré and Viviani (at sea, returning from their visit to St. Petersburg) did not help, but also felt that the French ambassador, Maurice Paléologue, was positively derelict in not acting to caution the Russians, in not urging restraint, and in failing to inform Paris immediately of the Russian decision to order general mobilization. In sum, France acted as an impetuous ally—with unfortunate consequences.

Italy: While not altogether comfortable with the style and manner of Italy's declaration of neutrality, Albertini asserted that it was justifiable: Austria-Hungary had acted unilaterally, Berlin and Vienna had failed to consult Rome, and thus the terms of the alliance were broken. He noted, however, that talk about a possible Habsburg territorial concession on Tretino meant Italy was willing to negotiate its entry—though Vienna never made an offer that could be discussed. Otherwise, Italy's role in 1914 was that of spectator.

Overall Conclusions: Albertini did not believe the war was inevitable, even after Sarajevo. He faulted Berlin and especially Bethmann for their incitement of Austria-Hungary; he recognized that Vienna had come to a fateful junction but believed that Berchtold should have accepted the "Halt in Belgrade" scheme as sufficient revenge. In

that sense Albertini reaffirmed the Versailles verdict that the Central Powers had the principle responsibility for the war, while not agreeing that they plotted or planned the war. He was also critical of Grey's lassitude, of the Russian decision for general mobilization, and of Serbia's irresponsibility before and after Sarajevo: each of these factors, when combined with German and Austro-Hungarian behavior, converted a "local" war into a World War. If no one willed the war, some were prepared to take great risks and others were prepared to hope for the best. In 1914 these attitudes and actions would not preserve the peace.

Samuel R. Williamson, Jr.

SOME OBSERVATIONS
ON THE HISTORICAL DEBATE
AT THE END OF THE 1950s

THE PUBLICATION of the translated Albertini volumes effectively marked the completion of one stage of historical debate about the origins of World War I. No other major studies were published during either the 1940s or 1950s. At the end of this period a "mild revisionist" version of the events of 1914 held sway, influenced by Fay but with some of Albertini's views clearly present. The Report of 1919 and Article 231 were considered to have maligned Berlin and Vienna unfairly. Although the two capitals bore the principal burden for the events of July 1914, other governments had also played parts in stoking the fires. The military in every country stood chastised, but especially the German High Command for its actions in July 1914 and in drafting the infamous Schlieffen Plan. The arms races, especially the Anglo-German

naval race, were thought to have conditioned the public and the governments to expect war while increasing tensions that might trigger it. Grey's failure to be more assertive was widely accepted as contributing to the disasters that summer. France should have been more restraining of its Russian ally, while St. Petersburg acted precipitately in mobilizing on July 30. Members of the Serbian bureaucracy were involved in the conspiracy to kill the archduke, but the exact extent of involvement remained obscure. Finally, it was widely accepted that no government had wanted a world war in the summer of 1914, though the German military were prepared to accept such a risk and the Austro-Hungarians were ready for a local war. In short, historians accepted Sidney Fay's assertion in 1928 that the "verdict of the Versailles Treaty that Germany and her allies were responsible for the War, in view of the evidence now available, is historically unsound."

By the end of the 1950s a veritable library of publications on the origins of World War I had appeared. Most of the major studies focused on diplomatic and strategic questions, reflecting the publication of diplomatic documents and memoir material. And much of the controversy had revolved around the issue of "war guilt" or "war responsibility"; after World War II this was, of course, no longer an issue of concern. At the same time valuable studies on economics, nationalism, imperialism, public opinion, and some features of military and naval policy had appeared, works of fundamental, "building-block" importance. But few works probed the connection between domestic issues and foreign policy with any structural care, and the archives remained closed to historians. Moreover, what had not taken place was also important. Although a group of German historians, headed by Gerhard Ritter, had subscribed in the early 1950s to a set of general declarations about 1914 that echoed many of the conclusions noted above, no major German historian had openly embraced an overall critique of German foreign policy made by many non-German scholars (including Fay). Certainly no German scholar had echoed the criticism advanced so profoundly by Luigi Albertini. Moderate or extreme revisionist views remained dominant in West German historical writing.

All of this was about to change in the early 1960s: German scholars would take the lead in reopening the debate, access to the archival sources would lead to surprising revelations for many countries, and a recasting of views and even of the conceptual framework for issues would result. A second stage in the historiography of World War I had begun.

II. NEW EVIDENCE AND NEW PERSPECTIVES: THE ERA OF FRITZ FISCHER AND AFTER

Fritz Fischer

BERLIN'S LUST FOR POWER

The publication in 1961 of *Griff nach der Weltmacht* (published in English as *Germany's Aims in the First World War*) came when Fritz Fischer was fifty-three years old. He was already an established professor at the University of Hamburg and a distinguished historian of early modern German history, and his resurrection of the issue of German war guilt came almost unexpectedly. Certainly it quickly opened anew the controversy of the 1920s and 1930s. From 1961 through the remainder of the decade Fischer, joined by his students and others, elaborated in lectures, articles, and document collections on the theme of German aggressiveness in 1914.

But Fischer's most detailed treatment of the outbreak of the war and of the continuity between Germany's pre-1914 behavior and its actions in July 1914 appeared in 1969. In *Krieg der Illusionen (War of Illusions)* the Hamburg professor argued that Germany not only risked war, even a world war that summer, but that it had planned to go to war since December 1912. Only the timing was in question; the shots fired at Sarajevo provided it with the opportunity to act. The analysis included here describes Germany's (and Bethmann Hollweg's) decisions first to back Austria-Hungary and then to press for belligerent action in 1914.

ON THE evening of the same day, 2nd July, Franz Joseph signed his letter to Wilhelm II which his special envoy, Count Hoyos, took to Berlin two days later and in which he said that the Monarchy proposed to eliminate Serbia as a political factor in the Balkans, to isolate it and to reduce it in size. . . .

Two days later, on 4th July, Austria-Hungary was again urged to take this very step. On that day the Vienna correspondent of the *Frankfurter Zeitung*, Ganz, on the instructions of the German ambassador, Tschirschky, said in the Foreign Ministry in Vienna that "Germany would support the Monarchy through thick and thin whatever the latter would decide about Serbia. . .the sooner Austria-Hungary started the better. Yesterday would have been better than today but today was better than tomorrow."

So as to leave no doubt about the determination of the German government ambassador Tschirschky confirmed this promise: "Even if the German press which today is totally anti-Serb were again to advocate peace Vienna must not allow itself to be confused. The Emperor and the Empire would certainly stand by Austria-Hungary. No Great Power could speak more frankly to another." Count Hoyos was therefore able to visit Berlin in the certain knowledge that Franz Joseph's inquiry which the Austrians had been encouraged by Berlin to make would receive a favourable reply. This inquiry which was contained in the letter written by the Emperor in his own hand and in a memorandum on a new Balkan policy for the Triple Alliance contained no definite military proposition for a war by Austria-Hungary against Serbia. . . . Instead the documents contained proposals for a long-term Balkan policy aimed at reducing Russia's influence in the Balkans by drawing Bulgaria into the Triple Alliance, by making Rumania abandon its growing friendship with Russia and Serbia, by reconciling Greece with Bulgaria and Turkey and by attracting it also to the Triple Alliance so as to isolate Serbia, the stronghold of anti-Austrian agitation. This regrouping could only be achieved if "Serbia. . .is eliminated as a political factor in the Balkans." There were no concrete proposals in the memorandum because it had been prepared before the murder of the Archduke. Its aim was to explain to the German ally the Austro-Hungarian view of the situation in the Balkans. After the assassination the memorandum was revised once more. More stress was now put on the arguments which emphasized the threat not just to Austria-Hungary but above all to Germany: "If Russia, assisted by France, tries to unite the Balkan states against Austria-Hungary, if it is anxious further to increase the strain which exists in the relationship with Rumania it is because this hostility is directed not just against the Monarchy as such, but no less against the ally of the German Empire, against the most vulnerable part of the central European bloc which is most exposed because of its geo-graphical situation and internal structure and which stands in the way of the realisation of Russia's world political plans." This was exactly what Wilhelm II thought. He was after all afraid that Germany's world position would be blocked by a pincer movement by the Franco-Russian alliance. . . .

As his ambassador in Vienna had done in the recent past, Wilhelm II exerted moral pressure on the Austrians to go to war with Serbia. That this was how his intervention was in fact seen in Vienna is shown by the comments which the Austrian Prime Minister, Stürgkh, made at the meeting of the joint ministerial council on 7th July in Vienna at which the Hungarian Prime Minister, Tisza, objected in vain that "it was not Germany's affair to judge whether or not we should now take action against Serbia."

Having studied the memorandum at the Foreign Ministry during the morning of 5th July, Bethmann Hollweg lectured the Emperor at Potsdam on the afternoon of the same day. He officially supported the Imperial assurance and thus gave it the constitutional sanction which the Austrian ambassador considered necessary. . . .

While the German government was determined from early July 1914 onwards to use this favourable opportunity for a war against France and Russia, the government in Vienna had decided on firm steps against Serbia but was looking for ways and means to avoid a military intervention by Russia although all ministers were convinced that this was impossible. At the meeting of the joint ministerial council in Vienna, held on 7th July after the return of Count Hoyos from Berlin, all ministers spoke in favour of getting even with Serbia. All those present with the exception of the Hungarian Prime Minister, Tisza, regarded a war against Serbia as the best solution even at the risk of Russian intervention. Tisza, however, was convinced that this was by no means a good moment for the Triple Alliance to fight a great war. He also insisted that after a war Serbia should be reduced in size but in deference to Russia should not be destroyed completely and that St. Petersburg should be reassured in this respect by guarantees.

The Chief of the General Staff, Conrad, who was present at various stages of the meeting to answer military questions, advocated an immediate war against Serbia and if necessary also against Russia. Berchtold, who had also expressed himself in favour of a war against Serbia, had doubts because of Rumania's likely behaviour and because of probable Italian compensation demands. But at the same time he was under very heavy German pressure. On 8th July Tschirschky called on him again to tell him "most emphatically" that "an action against Serbia was expected in Berlin." Berchtold understood from Tschirschky's remarks (this he told Tisza): "That in Germany any deal by us with Serbia would be interpreted as a confession of weakness which must have repercussions on our position in the Triple Alliance and on Germany's future policy." A similar fear had been voiced by the Austrian Prime Minister, Stürgkh, a day before at the meeting of the joint ministerial council: Austria ran "the risk that by a policy of hesitation and weakness it would later on no longer be so certain of Germany's unqualified support." On 9th July Berchtold observed that Franz Joseph also approved of energetic action against Serbia. He was "anxious that weak behaviour would discredit our position vis-à-vis Germany. . . ."

On 14th July at a meeting between Tisza, Stürgkh and Berchtold agreement was finally reached on the terms of the ultimatum to Serbia. Immediately after this meeting Tisza called on the German ambassador to inform him that he had changed his mind; he said that he too was now convinced of the need for a war against Serbia. But at the same time Tisza and also Berchtold told Tschirschky that the handing over of the ultimatum would be postponed until 25th July. They said that this delay had been decided upon so that the ultimatum would not be handed over precisely while the French President, Poincaré, was in St. Petersburg. Poincaré and Viviani were expected to pay a state visit to Russia after 20th July. Vienna did not want to provoke Russia unnecessarily and wanted to prevent the Russian and French statesmen from conferring immediately. But both Tisza and Berchtold emphasized to Tschirschky that the only reason for the delay was Poincaré's presence in St. Petersburg: "Berlin could rest completely assured. . .that there was no question of any hesitation or lack of resolution here." These almost timorous attempts to justify the delay show to what extent the Austro-Hungarian politicians felt pushed into a war against Serbia by the German government. For the same reason Berchtold also promised to send the final text of the note immediately—even before it had been submitted to Emperor Franz Joseph—to the German government for information.

At the meeting of the joint ministerial council in Vienna on 19th July the definitive text of the note was worked out and agreed. In addition it was decided that the forty-eight-hour ultimatum would be handed over in Belgrade on Thursday 23rd July at 5 p.m. To the council of ministers Berchtold justified the date with the argument that the Austro-Hungarian step would thereby probably not become known in St. Petersburg before Poincaré's departure. He was "definitely opposed to any further delay. . .as Berlin was getting nervous and news of our intentions had leaked out in Rome so that he could not guarantee that there would be no undesirable incidents if the affair was further postponed." But in spite of all assurances to the contrary Berlin was not completely sure that Vienna would stand firm. On the afternoon of 21st July Forgách, at the German ambassador's request, sent him the complete text of the note. On the morning of the same day Tschirschky had called at the Austrian Foreign Ministry and had thought it necessary to strengthen Vienna in its resolve. . . .

On Friday morning the ultimatum, delivered on Thursday afternoon (23rd July) in Belgrade, was published in the Viennese press and on the same day it was handed by the Austro-Hungarian ambassadors to the governments in the European capitals. The news struck like a bomb; because almost four weeks had passed since the assassination of the Archduke, the harshness of the demands was all the more striking and less comprehensible. The British Foreign Secretary, Sir Edward Grey, immediately tried to mediate so that the conflict between Austria and Serbia would not develop into a war between Austria and Russia and thus into a European war. . . .

In the afternoon of 24th July the Austrian ambassador in Belgrade received the Serb reply and departed at once. And this in spite of the fact that the Serb government had basically accepted the ultimatum with only a few reservations. In the evening preparations for the mobilisation against Serbia began in Vienna.

The British Foreign Minister continued his efforts to mediate in case of the threatening clash between Austria and Russia. When he was informed of the Serb reply he tried first to persuade Austria-Hungary to be content with it as a great diplomatic success. The German Foreign Ministry transmitted the suggestion to Vienna with the laconic observation that it had probably been overtaken by events. On Sunday 26th July Grey suggested a conference of the ambassadors of the four powers not involved in the conflict; they should seek to give Austria-Hungary satisfaction and thereby avoid a world war. Germany rejected this proposal also, on the grounds that it could not call Austria before a European court of justice. Instead the Foreign Ministry observed that steps for a direct understanding between St. Petersburg and Vienna were already afoot. On 27th July Grey had another conversation with Lichnowsky in which for the first time he voiced his suspicion that Germany was not seriously interested in mediation. While he, Grey, had continuously urged St. Petersburg to be conciliatory and while Serbia's very accommodating attitude was due to pressure from St. Petersburg, Germany had clearly not done all it could to persuade Vienna to be content with the Serb reply or at least to discuss it.

Lichnowsky concluded his report with the observation that in London "all the world" was convinced

that the key to the situation lies in Berlin and if peace is seriously wanted there Austria will be stopped from pursuing, as Sir Edward Grey puts it, a foolhardy policy.

Because of the hesitant and insufficiently purposeful behaviour of its ally Germany was now confronted with mediation offers which it did not wish to accept but which it could not reject outright without rousing world public opinion against it. Bethmann Hollweg wrote to Wilhelm II that if Germany rejected every role as mediator a limine "we would be seen by England and the whole world as responsible for the conflagration and as the real warmongers. On the one hand this would make it impossible for us to preserve the present good mood and on the other hand it would also deflect Britain from its neutrality."

To escape from this dilemma Bethmann Hollweg informed London that he had already initiated the desired mediation in Vienna. But in fact he merely sent on Lichnowsky's telegram to Vienna—without by the way the final comment—and appealed to the Vienna government to bear in mind Germany's difficult problem. The instruction to Tschirschky corresponded in content with the Chancellor's letter to the Emperor. It emphasized that "we [Germany] must give the impression of being forced into the war." Lest the government in Vienna doubted the determination of its German ally Jagow had called for the Austrian ambassador and prepared him for possible British mediation proposals. . . .After Austria-Hungary had at Germany's insistence declared war on Serbia on the next morning—28th July—Berchtold officially rejected the British proposal with diplomatic courtesy on the grounds that "as Germany is making this move a state of war already exists between the Monarchy and Serbia and that the Serb reply has therefore been overtaken by events." The declaration of war on Serbia had been decided on 27th July for 28th or 29th July "mainly to knock the bottom out of any attempt at intervention." Even before this Austrian action against Serbia had brought the outbreak of a European war closer still, feverish activity had begun in the various ministries in Berlin.

Moltke, Waldersee and Tirpitz had returned to Berlin on 26th July, the Emperor on 27th July. Immediately, on 26th July, Moltke had sent the draft of the ultimatum to Belgium for examination and information to the Foreign Ministry. Mobilisation orders for the civil authorities were also prepared for signature by the Emperor. After his return from the North Sea cruise Admiral von Müller summed up his impressions of the situation in Berlin as follows:

Tendency of our policy: keep quiet, letting Russia put herself in the wrong, but then not shying away from war.

The Austro-Hungarian Naval Attaché in Berlin had the same impression on 27th July as well. He wrote

that people here await all possible complications with the utmost calm and regard the moment as very favourable for a big settlement.

Neither the Foreign Ministry nor the General Staff were very happy about the Emperor's early return [from the North Sea voyage] because it was feared that Wilhelm II might confuse the government's carefully planned scheme with proposals of his own. This was in fact what happened; when the text of the Serb reply was presented to the Emperor, though only on the morning of 28th July, he thought that this note was a Serb "capitulation of the most humiliating kind" and declared: "because of it there no longer exists *any reason for war.*" Because this would mean that the Austro-Hungarian army would for the third time have been mobilised in vain against Serbia, the Emperor proposed that as a *satisfaction d'honneur* Austria should occupy various areas in Serbia as a pledge until definite assurances had been received by [from, *sic*] Serbia that it would behave itself in [the, *sic*] future. This idea which was on the same lines as the British Foreign Secretary's "pledge proposal" of 29th July was transmitted belatedly and altered by Bethmann Hollweg. He did not pass the proposal on to Vienna as coming from the Emperor, nor did he mention the latter's preparedness to mediate

between Austria and Serbia, but suggested using the pledge proposal as a basis for talks with St. Petersburg because Austria-Hungary could not actively take military action against Serbia before 12th August and would in the meantime remain exposed to mediation attempts from other cabinets. That Bethmann Hollweg's suggestions to Germany's ally were more designed to produce a favourable constellation for the European war than to prevent this war becomes clear from his demand that it was

imperative that the responsibility for the eventual spread of the conflict to those not directly concerned should in all circumstances fall on Russia. . . .

The Russian Foreign Minister, Sazonov, had also made various proposals in the days after relations were broken off between Austria and Serbia. He tried to find a compromise which would preserve Russia's prestige but which would satisfy Austria without depriving Serbia altogether of its independence. His proposals were so numerous that they seemed almost confusing as the latest was quickly followed by another. In London it was feared that "the rapid succession of fresh proposals and suggestions coming from St. Petersburg makes it easier for Germany to find fresh excuses for her inactivity." At the same time Sazonov tried to convince the German ambassador, Pourtalès, that Germany must make its influence felt in Vienna and he invited him to make proposals which he, Sazonov, would then take up.

At the same time Russia began military preparations. The Petersburg government was determined from the beginning of the crisis, from the time the Austrian ultimatum was delivered in Belgrade, to go to war against Austria-Hungary if Serbia was threatened with total destruction. . . .

The Austrian declaration of war on Serbia had led to a substantial shift in the balance in St. Petersburg between the military and the political factors. Austria-Hungary had proved finally that it was set on war against Serbia. Its German ally appeared to be the moving force behind this decision. Any further delay in the slow process of mobilisation meant a dangerous loss of time for Russia, because Germany could mobilise with lightning speed.

From the evening of 28th July onwards not only the military but also the Foreign Minister tried to convince the Tsar of the need for total mobilisation. . . .

Partial mobilisation meant for Russia *de facto* the same risk as a general mobilisation. If Russia mobilised partially and there was a war with Austria-Hungary it would not be prepared at all for the war that was certain to start with Germany. The fear that the German government was in fact gravitating towards such a war grew daily in the period between 24th and 30th July. Sazonov continually received evidence of the intransigence of Berlin and Vienna.

Russia's responsibility cannot therefore be said to lie in the fact that on 30th July the Russian government decided to transform the partial mobilisation into a general one; it can be held responsible because it refused to stand by while Serbia was destroyed and it was itself completely pushed out of the Balkans, that is forced to give up hope of the Straits. Russia's share of responsibility for the outbreak of the war in the summer of 1914 lies in the fact that it adhered to this principle of Russian policy, not in the fact that it decided on 30th July to proclaim a general mobilisation.

Even after this the Russian government continued to hope for a peaceful settlement, particularly as direct talks with Vienna appeared to start again on 31st July.

An examination of Russia's attitude in the July crisis and of its motives therefore shows plainly that Russia tried to the end to prevent the war. . . .

The tension in Berlin reached its climax in the late afternoon of 29th July; after the Austrian declaration of war on Serbia and the shelling of Belgrade the only news received was that of the partial mobilisation of the four southern military districts, in spite of all the threats from St. Petersburg that Russia could not stand by and watch the Austrian provocations. The General Staff

and the Ministry of War urged that the important gain in time should not be wasted and insisted that Germany should immediately proclaim a state of imminent war. In addition it was also probable that if a decision was not taken soon in St. Petersburg the Austrian army corps would march alone against Serbia and remain in a defensive position on the Galician-Russian frontier; this meant a serious danger to the Schlieffen Plan which relied on Austria's advance against Russia.

The Chancellor and the Foreign Ministry were certainly not opposed to this idea. But it remained their main objective to give Russia the role of the attacker so as not unnecessarily to burden the domestic and international position of the German Empire. The Bavarian ambassador in Vienna, Freiherr von Tucher, for example, reported rumours that the Chancellor had expressed himself against an ultimatum to St. Petersburg, "as Russia and also Britain see in such a step a challenge, and the latter power whose neutrality is valued very highly could thus be brought on to Russia's side."

At the Crown Council on the afternoon of 29th July in Potsdam, at which the proclamation of the state of imminent war was discussed, the question of British neutrality in this war was also considered in detail. Wilhelm II was convinced that Britain would remain neutral. The English King had promised this to his brother, Prince Heinrich, who had just returned from Britain. The doubts expressed by Secretary of State Tirpitz who was also present were brushed aside by the Emperor with the remark: "I have the word of a king, that is enough for me." After Bethmann Hollweg's return from the meeting in Potsdam he attempted, probably because the military were pressing for the military time-table to be preserved, to reap the fruits of his many years' wooing of the British. He asked the British ambassador to call on him in the Chancellery and offered him a German-British neutrality agreement for the impending war of Germany and Austria against Russia and France; in return he held out to the British government the assurance that Germany would not touch

France's territorial integrity. To a question by the ambassador on the French colonies Bethmann Hollweg gave no firm reply.

Had Bethmann Hollweg known that at this very moment the Foreign Ministry was decoding a report from Lichnowsky containing a clear warning from Grey that if Germany attacked France Britain could in no circumstances remain neutral, he would undoubtedly not have made this move which revealed the intentions of the German government.

Lichnowsky's news had an alarming effect in the Foreign Ministry particularly as the Chancellor had stuck his neck out so far in his talk with Goschen. But Lichnowsky's telegram did not change the German government's decision to go to war. Given the distribution of power in Berlin the Chancellor and the Foreign Ministry could not have gone back on the decision even if they had now not wanted the war. Instead Bethmann Hollweg tried immediately, in the night of 29th to 30th July, to persuade the Austrians not to reject all mediation offers too curtly. Tschirschky was instructed to urge Berchtold not to reject out of hand Grey's last proposal for mediation by the four powers not directly concerned. In a further telegram Tschirschky was invited to draw Berchtold's attention to a second mediation possibility, namely a direct exchange of views between Vienna and St. Petersburg, the rejection of which by Vienna had greatly disturbed Grey. . . .

The same night Moltke also sent a telegram to Vienna. He informed his Austrian colleague, Conrad von Hoetzendorf, that *partial* Russian mobilisation was no reason for German mobilisation but that Germany must wait for a state of war between Russia and Austria-Hungary. Moltke gave the instruction "Do not declare war on Russia but wait for Russia's attack." The military and the civil leadership were therefore unanimous in their demand that Austria should in no circumstances appear as the aggressor but that it must be left to Russia to take the decisive step which would lead to war.

By next morning the excitement in the Foreign Ministry over Lichnowsky's alarming telegram had given way once more to sober calm. Although hopes of British neutrality had been seriously shaken renewed attention was paid to the idea that Britain might be kept neutral, at least during the beginning stages of the war. If Russia appeared obviously as the attacker in the impending war it would be impossible for the British government to persuade the majority in Parliament to join in the war on the side of Russia. It was with this line of thought in mind that Tschirschky was now instructed to induce Berchtold to show willingness to negotiate so that Russia, whose general mobilisation was expected hourly in Berlin, would be blamed for the war which would then break out.

On the morning of 30th July Bethmann Hollweg drafted a telegram for Wilhelm II to send to the Tsar. The Chancellor's purpose was to describe the probable consequences of Russian mobilisation and thus to make the Tsar responsible for all that would ensue while presenting Germany as prepared to negotiate to the last. But the Emperor, embittered by Russia's partial mobilisation of which he was not informed until the morning of 30th July and by the "betrayal" of the British, that "miserable lot of shopkeepers," had already firmly refused to go on playing the mediator. For this reason Bethmann Hollweg appealed to Wilhelm II's instincts as a statesman by prophesying that "this telegram will become a particularly important document for history."

The Chancellor sent a telegram to London saying that the Austro-Hungarian readiness for negotiation was considerably endangered by the continuing Russian and French military preparations. With this the Chancellor tried to prepare the ground in Britain so that Russia could be presented as responsible for starting the war, even if it continued to delay the proclamation of total mobilisation.

Bethmann Hollweg, Moltke and Falkenhayn held a meeting [on July 30th] shortly after 9 p.m. at which the military successfully insisted that a state of "imminent danger of war" should be proclaimed not later than the following morning, 31st July—a step which in Germany inevitably brought with it mobilisation. With this decision, taken before news of the Russian general mobilisation was received, Berlin had fixed the beginning of the war for the first days of August even without the government being driven to this by Russia's general mobilisation. By postponing for fifteen hours the start of the mobilisation measures the Chancellor had at any rate gained a little time in which the Russian government might yet take a step which would put it in the wrong in the eyes of the world and allow him to go on with his original plan.

At about 11 p.m. the first rumors did in fact arrive in Berlin that the Russians had ordered a general mobilisation. Bethmann Hollweg immediately asked for his instructions to Tschirschky to be cancelled by telephone and telegram.

Once Russia had become the villain of the piece as the result of this order there was no longer any need for Bethmann Hollweg to pretend that he was trying to help with the peace mediation. Later, after the controversy had started between Austria-Hungary and Germany over the war guilt question, Tschirschky, commenting on a private letter by Jagow, who had said that Austria-Hungary's intransigence had been responsible for the start of the war, denied that this had been so and maintained that the Russian mobilisation had been the cause:

I was personally requested by telephone (by Herr von Stumm) immediately to cease all mediation activity in Vienna *because* news of the Russian mobilisation had just been received.

In the course of that same night Tschirschky was informed of the decision of the conference of military and civil leaders in Berlin that Germany would present Russia with an ultimatum because of the mobilisation measures. Early on the morning of 31st July the ambassador gave this important news to the Austro-Hungarian Foreign Minister.

The issue discussed at this conference in Berlin shortly before midnight after the receipt of the first news of the Russian general mobilisation was the German mobilisation. The military pressed for an immediate decision; Bethmann Hollweg on the other hand asked for the mobilisation to be delayed until the Russians had rejected the German ultimatum. The Quartermaster-General, Waldersee, said in a letter to Jagow of 1st July 1926 about Moltke:

With us, his collaborators until the outbreak of the war, he had agreed that he would insist only on the mobilisation, then the war would start of its own accord; a declaration by us would only do harm.

As Bethmann Hollweg has attested in a letter to Jagow of August 1919, Moltke was not only in favour of an immediate mobilisation but of starting military operations at the same time. But the Chancellor's view prevailed, that if military action was taken without an announcement then there was no reason for issuing an ultimatum to Belgium—"that was why we decided on our ultimatum telegram to Pourtalès"—and that otherwise—as he put it to Ballin—"he could not carry the Socialists with him."

This night the Chancellor therefore once more managed to assert himself against the military and to get a hearing for his arguments in favour of a perfect preparation for the opening of the war. The decision to announce the "state of imminent war" on the afternoon of 31st July was upheld. The proclamation of German mobilisation on the other hand was delayed for one more day. First Russia would be sent an ultimatum to stop its mobilisation. One of the reasons why Bethmann Hollweg obtained this last postponement was that his prophecy that Russia could be given the role of the aggressor seemed at last to be coming true.

Following this second meeting on 30th July Moltke sent a telegram to the Austrian Chief of Staff giving him the go ahead:

Wait for Russian mobilisation; Austria must be preserved, must mobilise immediately against Russia, Germany will mobilise. Italy must be compelled by compensations to fulfil its alliance obligations.

A similar telegram was sent off simultaneously by the Austro-Hungarian military attaché in Berlin after a meeting with Moltke. It contained the following additional directives:

> Reject the new move by England to preserve the peace. Perseverance with the European war is the last means to preserve Austria-Hungary. Germany is definitely taking part.

Like Tschirschky who had been given instructions to pass on to the Austro-Hungarian Foreign Ministry, Conrad was now also told not to make any further mediation moves. On this point there was therefore unanimity between the civil and military leadership in Germany. It was spelt out very clearly in these telegrams that Germany demanded an Austro-Hungarian mobilisation against Russia, relegating the Austrian war against Serbia to second place; Bethmann Hollweg in fact said to Vienna the following afternoon: "We expect from Austria immediate *active* participation in the war against Russia. . . ."

On the afternoon of Friday 31st July, the British ambassador, Goschen, delivered the British government's rejection of the German call for British neutrality. Not for a moment—Goschen told the Chancellor—had the British government considered the German proposal. Britain would not commit itself to stand by inactively "while French colonies are taken and France is beaten."

> From the material point of view such a proposal is unacceptable, for France could be so crushed as to lose her position as a Great Power, and became [sic] subordinate to German policy without further territory in Europe being taken from her.

Nor could the British government agree to bargain over its obligations and interests as regards the neutrality of Belgium.

Bethmann Hollweg received this news without saying a word. It seemed to the ambassador as if the Chancellor was so preoccupied with the news about Russian military activities on the German frontier that he was not able immediately to take in the full meaning of the British answer. Instead of replying to it he tried to explain to the British ambassador the dangerous military and political situation of the German Empire. While Germany had preached moderation and peace Russia had mobilised against Austria.

> If now the news he had received proved true and military measures were also being taken against Germany, he could not remain quiet, as he would not leave his country defenseless while other Powers were gaining time.

Bethmann Hollweg indicated to the ambassador

> that in a very short time, perhaps even today, they would have to take some serious step. .

The Chancellor was anxious to make it clear to the British government that Russia was responsible for the war and that Germany was only reacting to Russian provocation. The French ambassador, Cambon, noticed that to him the Chancellor did not complain about the Russian mobilisation. From this Cambon concluded "that the only reason for approaching London is the hope of preventing a British intervention."

When at 12 noon the Russian general mobilisation was officially announced, and at the same time the Austrians proclaimed total mobilisation, all military and diplomatic schemes prepared in Berlin began to be implemented according to plan. The appeals to Vienna to pretend willingness to negotiate had already stopped abruptly the previous night. Also on the morning of 31st July Berlin ceased to consider the mediation question any further, whereas feverish activity was displayed in London, St. Petersburg, Paris and even in Vienna in a last-minute effort to prevent the outbreak of the great European war.

At 1 p.m. the "state of imminent war" was declared in Berlin. Wilhelm II and Bethmann Hollweg justified these measures in solemn and moving speeches to the nation with the *leitmotif* that Russia had forced the war on the German nation. . . .

On Saturday, 1st August the Bundesrat met at 12 noon. The Chairman, Bethmann Hollweg, requested the approval of the states for a war with Russia and France. He explained that this war was imminent even though the replies of Russia and France to the German ultimata had not yet been received. The states gave their consent. They had no choice anyway, having been confronted with *faits accomplis*. In Bethmann Hollweg's review of the events of the recent past there is a clear tendency to blame Russia for the war. The Russian mobilisation had come in the middle of the mediation activities and as a result war had been forced on the German Empire. The Chancellor did not mention England in this speech, probably so as not to worry the Bundesrat, or possibly because at that moment he did not think that Britain would intervene immediately because Russia appeared to be obviously responsible for the war.

The view that Russia's general mobilisation was the factor responsible for the start of the war was given out also to the press by the chief of the press section of the Foreign Ministry, Hammann, on 1st August. The Emperor and the German nation were presented as determined opponents of preventive wars. Germany had tried unceasingly with Britain to find a peaceful solution.

Russia alone forces a war on Europe which nobody has wanted except Russia; the full force of responsibility falls on Russia alone.

This line was also taken consistently in the German White Book on the war of 2nd August and by Bethmann Hollweg in his Reichstag speech of 4th August.

The real state of affairs in Berlin was however very different from the picture which Hammann tried to convey to the foreign press of an Emperor in despair because of the war and a German government unhappy over the failure of the peace negotiations. The Chief of the General Staff, Moltke, had pleasant memories of 1st August: "There was, as I said, an atmosphere of happiness." And Admiral von Müller wrote in his diary on 1st August:

The morning papers carry the speeches of the Emperor and of the Chancellor to the enthusiastic crowd assembled outside the Palace and the Chancellor's palais respectively. *The mood is brilliant. The government has managed brilliantly to make us appear the attacked.*

On 1st August at 12:52 p.m. the declaration of war on Russia was sent off, which Pourtalès was to hand over if the answer to the German ultimatum was negative or not forthcoming. At 5 p.m. the German mobilisation order was officially issued. . . .

Uncertainty as to whether Pourtalès had handed over the German declaration of war in St. Petersburg and whether Germany was officially at war led to a very excited meeting in Berlin on Sunday, 2nd August, on the possible declaration of war on France which in turn was regarded as a prerequisite for the ultimatum to Belgium and the invasion of that country. The state of war with Russia would have enabled the German government to justify the declaration of war on France with the Russo-French military alliance. The French government did not allow itself to be provoked into a military reaction by the ultimatum. When the German ambassador, Schoen, collected the reply to the ultimatum on 1st August at 1 p.m. Prime Minister Viviani was cleverly evasive and said that France would do what its interests demanded. In the afternoon, at 5 p.m., France announced its mobilisation but kept its troops ten kilometres from the frontier. The German government regarded this reply as "ambiguous and unsatisfactory" but could not use it as the basis for a declaration of war as it was not yet certain that the war between Germany and Russia had formally begun. Therefore it was claimed as early as the following day, Sunday, 2nd August, that France had committed military acts on German soil. In the night of 2nd to 3rd August Britain was informed of this so as to give the impression that Germany had been attacked and to make it more difficult for the British government to join in the war on the side of France. "According to absolutely reliable information," it was said, "France has committed the following violations against us:

1. French cavalry patrols have today in the early afternoon crossed the frontier at Altmünsterol in Alsace.
2. A French air force officer has been shot down near Wesel.
3. Two Frenchmen have tried to blow up the Kochem tunnel at the Moselle railway and were shot in the attempt.
4. French infantry has crossed the frontier in Alsace and has opened fire."

These "frontier violations" were presented by the Foreign Ministry as proof "that Germany, having stood for the idea of peace to the utmost limits of the possible, is being pushed by its opponent into the role of the challenged party which in order to preserve its existence *must* take up arms." As early as the evening of 2nd August the Secretary at the German embassy in London, von Schubert, had in accordance with his instructions presented information to the Foreign Office designed to prove the violation of Belgian and Dutch neutrality by France, so as to justify to Britain this breach of neutrality by Germany. Eyre Crowe said this statement sounded like a joke. But Schubert "indignantly declared that the matter was most serious, as the statement emanated from his government itself."

On 3rd August the German ambassador in Paris was instructed to inform the French government at 6 p.m. that because of the French frontier violations Germany considered a state of war to exist with France. . . .

Neutral Luxemburg was occupied on 2nd August and German troops marched into Belgium on the morning of 4th August. The violation of Belgian neutrality had been particularly carefully prepared. As early as 29th July, the day on which news of Russia's partial mobilisation had been received in Berlin, the ultimatum to Belgium which Moltke had transmitted to the Foreign Ministry immediately after his return from leave on 26th July was handed in a sealed envelope to the German ambassador in Brussels with the order to open the letter only on receipt of telegraphic instruction. This was given on 2nd August for the same day at 8 p.m. German time.

The communication assumed that war was imminent between France and Germany. It was claimed that France intended to march through Belgian territory so that it was "a dictate of self-preservation for Germany" to anticipate the French attack. As Belgium would not be able to resist the French advance without assistance the Belgian government could not regard it as a hostile act if Germany as part of its opposition to its enemies would "also. . .enter Belgian territory." For the case that Belgium was prepared to tolerate the German invasion without opposition Germany made all sorts of promises regarding Belgian integrity and independence as well as compensation payments. But if Belgium offered armed resistance or made the German advance difficult by the destruction of railways, tunnels, etc., Belgium would be regarded as an enemy and "the subsequent settlement of the relationship between the two states be left to be decided by force of arms." For Moltke, in distinction to Bethmann Hollweg, the ultimatum to Belgium served to provoke France. He expected the news of this ultimatum to Belgium to arouse such popular feeling in France that the government would be compelled immediately to send troops into Belgium. France would than in fact, as the ultimatum envisaged, be guilty of a violation of Belgian neutrality before Germany.

Because of the pressing German timetable the period of twenty-four hours originally scheduled for a reply to the ultimatum was reduced to twelve hours. On the morning of 3rd August, after the period had run out, the Belgian government rejected the German demand and announced that it intended to "oppose by force any violation of Belgian neutrality."

In London the Cabinet met on 2nd August—an unheard-of break with the tradition by which the weekend was sacrosanct. Grey was to address the Commons the following day. The Cabinet therefore discussed the statements which the Foreign Secretary would make to the House. The first issue was the intervention of the British navy to protect the French coast against an attack by the German fleet. A statement was agreed which Grey handed to the French ambassador, Cambon, the same evening.

Secondly the Cabinet discussed what the British attitude would be if the neutrality of Belgium was violated by Germany; agreement on this point was not, however, reached until the following day. The question was whether a German invasion of Belgium automatically constituted a *casus belli* for Britain. The overwhelming majority of the Cabinet was in favour of an immediate declaration of war in such an eventuality.

Before Grey addressed the Commons on the afternoon of 3rd August he had already been told by Lichnowsky that Germany would march into Belgium. At the same time the German ambassador had assured him that Germany would "fully respect" Belgium's integrity "after the conclusion of the campaign. . .and make full restitution for the requisitions and the damage done by us." In

the Commons Grey described the violation of Belgian neutrality and the danger of an outright French defeat as irreconcilable with British interests. With this line of argument he convinced and united Parliament including the Irish parties.

On the evening of this important day the British Cabinet decided to ask Germany whether the German government was prepared, as the French government had already done, to give a firm assurance that it would respect Belgian neutrality. The ultimatum was sent off on 4th August at 2 p.m. and a reply was asked for by midnight. . . .

When Bethmann Hollweg and Jagow regretted that they could give no other answer than that which they had previously given to Goschen, the British ambassador, in accordance with his instructions, asked for his passport and stated that after midnight central European time Britain regarded itself as being at war with Germany.

Fritz Stern

BETHMANN HOLLWEG AND THE WAR: THE LIMITS OF RESPONSIBILITY

The part played by Chancellor Bethmann Hollweg—his views, his actions, his failure to act—is one of the main themes of Fritz Fischer's assessment of Germany's pre-war and wartime diplomacy. The German chancellor has subsequently (since 1961) been the object of intensive historical scrutiny, much of it defining and clarifying issues. One such effort was Fritz Stern's essay, "Bethmann Hollweg and the War: The Limits of Responsibility." The Seth Low Professor of History at Columbia University and author of *The Politics of Cultural Despair* and *Gold and Iron: Bismarck, Bleichröder, and the Building of the German Empire,* Stern sought to remind historians of two important facts: first, that there are pressures upon those who hold public office; and second, that there are

"Bethmann Hollweg and the War: The Limits of Responsibility" by Fritz Stern, from *The Responsibility of Power* edited by Leonard Krieger and Fritz Stern, pp. 271-272, 274-288. Copyright © 1967 by Doubleday & Company, Inc. Reprinted by permission of the publisher.

limits on what an individual can and cannot achieve in government. His account is thus more sympathetic and less critical of the senior civilian official in Wilhelmine Germany. It is also a careful reminder that government is more complex and motivation less clear than historians often suggest. The reader must decide whether Fischer or Stern offers the more realistic picture of the German chancellor in the summer of 1914.

BETHMANN Hollweg, philosopher-bureaucrat, a riddle to his contemporaries, has remained a subject of unending controversy for historians. His responsibility for the outbreak of the First World War and for Germany's conduct of it has been polemically debated for decades. A villain to the Allies, to the German military and their Pan-German allies, he was a weakling and the country's gravedigger. After 1918, German nationalist historians blamed his indecision and defeatism for hobbling Germany's war effort. His few defenders in the 1920s insisted that he had been a "military Chancellor," only more reticent and circumspect than the Pan-German extremists. The Third Reich interrupted the argument which, a few years ago, Fritz Fischer's massive *Griff nach der Weltmacht* revived. The roles have been reversed: Bethmann Hollweg's detractors now claim that he was an annexationist with philosophical veneer, and his defenders suggest that he was a noble, ill-cast bureaucrat, with occasional annexationist leanings. . . .

The controversy is more than an academic exercise about an inscrutable individual. Bethmann Hollweg, Imperial Germany's last effective chancellor, led Germany into the First World War and left his office only after unrestricted submarine warfare and America's entry into the war had all but sealed Germany's fate. He necessarily is at the focus of all discussions concerning Germany's war guilt in 1914, her war aims during the war, and of the debate but recently started concerning the continuity of German history in the twentieth century. His chancellorship illuminates as well the mounting internal antagonisms of the Bismarckian Reich. The study of Bethmann, then, has ever been controversial, important, and politically explosive. . . .

Theobald von Bethmann Hollweg, born in 1856, was a Prussian by birth, not tradition. His ancestors on the paternal side were rich merchants and bankers in Frankfurt; his grandfather became a professor of law in Prussia and in the liberal era under Prince William a Prussian minister. He resigned his post at the beginning of the constitutional conflict in 1862. Bismarck's political adventurism revolted him, and a few hours before the outbreak of the Austro-Prussian war, he wrote the King, imploring him to remove the reckless Bismarck. Time would be when Bismarck would be celebrated as the cautious statesman and Bethmann's grandson censured as the devious aggressor. Theobald's mother was a Swiss, Isabella de Rougemont. He was born on an estate his father had bought in Hohenfinow in the Mark Brandenburg; born in the Mark, but not wholly of it.

He studied jurisprudence, entered the civil service at the age of twenty-five, and in 1905 was named Prussian Minister of the Interior. In 1909 the Emperor appointed him Bülow's successor as Chancellor—and Bethmann had seen enough of politics in Imperial Germany to know the complexities and limitations of that office.

In fact, Imperial Germany could hardly be governed. Time and Bismarck had created a system of checks and imbalances, destined not to work. The political structure was cumbersone at best: a federal system in which Prussia held a central, but not unchallenged, position. The pseudo-constitutional state hid the locus of sovereignty. William, despite his occasional, disastrous outbursts of autocracy, had neither the constitutional prerogative nor the personal capacity to govern Germany. Parliaments, elected according to different systems of suffrage and therefore unequally representative, did not control the executive, though parliamentary approval was needed for the enactment of budgets and laws. The Chancellor's tenure was on the Emperor's sufferance; he was directly responsible to the Crown and indirectly dependent on the Reichstag which reflected the social composition—and cleavages—of an industrialized Germany. In theory, the Chancellor had to translate the Emperor's will—and sometimes whim—into effective political action, and when necessary, obtain parliament's approval. In practice, the Chancellor was caught between the conservative classes which, economically declining, were desperately clinging to their positions of power, and the liberal and radical groups, representative of a new society, that sought greater recognition of their own steadily increasing popular strength. The political system, already intricate and often unwieldy under Bismarck, had become incompatible with the social realities of the new age.

Bethmann's task was hard and his authority severely restricted. Political power had become much more fragmented after Bismarck's dismissal. The Chancellor had to contend with the military and naval leaders of the Reich who, fortified by their direct access to the Emperor, claimed not only autonomy in their *ressorts* but a strong voice in foreign policy as well. Antiquated court factions and modern pressure groups also sought to wield power or shape policy. In the years before the Great War, Germany faced immense problems at home and abroad. Internally, her industrial power provoked a steadily deepening antagonism between declining authoritarianism and a growing democratic movement. Externally, Germany's might aroused the fears of her neighbors, and her fitful, bullying policy, partly caused by her internal dissension, heightened these fears. Germany's worst problem was that its political system was virtually paralyzed and incapable of coping with these problems.

Bethmann intended to pursue a conciliatory course at home and abroad. He hoped to find a diagonal line, as he often put it, between conservative and liberal-radical pressures. "A clear conservative policy in the Reich was in fact an impossibility—the Right knew that best of all," he wrote after the war. A consistently liberal policy, enhancing the power of the Reichstag, would have been equally impossible—for the Kaiser would not have tolerated it and the Reichstag could not have mustered a workable majority. Bethmann pushed meek measures meekly: he tried, for example, to reform the antiquated electoral system in Prussia which was the parliamentary bulwark of feudal dominance and as such sacrosanct to the conservatives and anathema to the left. He failed, inevitably, and in the process deeply antagonized both sides, also inevitably. He realized—as did most intelligent contemporaries—that the integration of the proletariat into the nation was the principal requirement of the age, but he saw no way of achieving it. In the years before the war, the antagonisms instead waxed stronger, and the opposing groups pushed each other into more radical and recalcitrant positions, as they did again during the war. The Socialists scored a great electoral triumph in 1912; a year later, the military flaunted their contempt for the *Rechtsstaat* in the Zabern affair, and enjoyed the Chancellor's full backing.

Germany's external position was also precarious. The dangers were far more real than those Bismarck invoked to rally nation and Reichstag for military expenditures, and Bethmann always managed to obtain increasing army and navy appropriations. Foreign danger was sometimes a domestic convenience. It was always a source of the deepest worry to Bethmann who, unlike his predecessors, had had no military or diplomatic experience. The danger of war had mounted steadily since 1905, especially since the Bosnian crisis of 1908. Bethmann realized that Germany's exposed position between France and Russia had been rendered still more dangerous by its *Weltpolitik* and by its naval ambitions which had prompted England to seek closer ties with

France and Russia. He found no comfort in Tirpitz's promises that his navy would frighten England into neutrality or negotiations, and in either case remove it as a threat to Germany in case of war. Instead he found England supporting France in the second Moroccan crisis and he heard with dismay of the Anglo-French naval conversations of 1912. His fear of German encirclement was genuine. He saw Germany, with decrepit Austria its only ally, surrounded by a ring of enemies, ready to block its continued growth. Bethmann certainly shared the nation's claustrophobia. He, too, had abandoned Bismarck's premise that Germany was a satiated power, and had embraced that curious blend of contradictory beliefs—social Darwinism, misunderstood romanticism, and cultural pessimism—all pointing to German expansion as the only alternative to stagnation. In January 1912, for example, he spoke privately of a great colonial empire in Africa, which Germany would be able to organize out of the Belgian Congo and the Dutch and Portuguese colonies. Later that year, during the Balkan wars that clearly involved and damaged Austrian interests, he declared before the Reichstag: "If our allies while asserting their interests should against all expectations be attacked by a third party, then we would have to come resolutely to their aid. And then we would fight for the maintenance of our own position in Europe and in defense of our future and security." Germany's future in Bethmann's eyes, to say nothing of his colleagues', had to be open and dynamic, commensurate with its steadily growing economic power. Bethmann rejected the idea of a preventive war, but was determined to safeguard this expansionist future by all means, including war.

Germany's diplomatic position deteriorated during his tenure. At the time of the Haldane mission, he was already afraid of an Anglo-Russian naval convention, which would tighten the ring around Germany still more. He was ready to slow down German naval construction in return for a political agreement virtually involving an English withdrawal from Europe, giving Germany a free hand. Despite the failure of the Haldane

mission, Anglo-German relations improved during the Balkan crisis. Austria's position, on the other hand, grew still more precarious and her reliability as an ally declined accordingly. The specter of an isolated Germany, gradually overshadowed by an ambitious, rapidly industrializing Russia, with its appalling multitudes, allied to France and probably England, haunted Bethmann and all German leaders.

Bethmann knew that in many quarters he was held responsible for Germany's mounting difficulties. In an age of national bombast and impetuosity, his plodding caution and conciliatoriness won grudging acceptance at best.

Berlin wits already called him *Bethmann soll Weg* (Bethmann should go), and there were always rumors of his impending ouster. The Crown Prince detested him, and the Kaiser, though respectful of him at most times and aware that he needed him, often railed against his *Schlappheit,* his brooding, and his philosophical airs. William's contempt for diplomats and civil servants was universally known, even if particularly crude outbursts against "stupid and anxiety-ridden diplomats, indeed [against] stupid civilians generally" did not always make the rounds. The Kaiser preferred the often brainless virility, the *Schneidigkeit,* of soldiers. In this, too, he epitomized his age. Though tiresomely repeated, it is nevertheless true— and important to an understanding of Bethmann—that Germany was a thoroughly militaristic country in the years before the war. Gerhard Ritter cites one revealing instance: "It became good form even for higher state officials to wear military uniform at every conceivably fitting occasion. Thus Bethmann Hollweg in his first appearance as chancellor in the Reichstag appeared in a major's uniform—an exercise for which Bismarck with his endless masquerading as *Kürassiergeneral* certainly was not blameless. Only the person who could wear the uniform with the silver epaulettes counted as a real man [*ganzer Kerl*]."

Outwardly Bethmann accepted the values of this system of creeping militarism, though he probably realized the attendant danger of eroding civilian control and political reason. At the same time, it seems probable that this exaltation of things military must have grated on his sensitive civilian soul.

It is generally agreed that Bethmann's abiding sense of responsibility and his brooding over every decision were his outstandingly attractive traits. What a contrast there was between the unevenly ebullient Kaiser, ever boastful of German prowess, so representative of his age, and Bethmann, the enigmatic, taciturn worrier! The slippery, smiling Bülow had certainly been more attuned to William's age and personality than his successor. As Riezler noted: "The Chancellor [was, sic] a child of the first half of the nineteenth century and of a better education [Bildung]. Strange that he with his old humanistic convictions, his seriousness, and his incapacity for all sham should have gained power in the new German milieu and should have been able to hold his own against parliamentarians and jobbers."

The stark contrast in style and character between Bethmann and almost all the other leaders of Imperial Germany had encouraged the belief that there was a fundamental divergence of political aims as well. For this, however, the general consensus about Germany's national destiny was too broad and the Kaiser's tolerance for dissent too narrow: Bethmann Hollweg, as we will see, was perspicacious in his worries about Germany's course, but he had no alternative to propose and would have been powerless to implement one.

Bethmann resisted all efforts at the diminution of his office, and particularly all efforts to enhance the power of state secretaries. He had difficulties with his own appointee, Kiderlen-Wächter, who liked to conduct his foreign negotiations without informing him. Bethmann successfully resisted even the Kaiser's encroachments: in March 1912, at the time of the Anglo-German talks, William, impatient with what he thought Bethmann's dilatoriness, gave important orders directly to the ambassador in London and to the war minister in Berlin. Bethmann replied by submitting his resigna-

tion, warning the Emperor against a precipitous policy that in the end might force Germany into an attack on France in which the victim, but not the aggressor, would have the support of its allies. Bethmann argued that he could not take the responsibility for such a policy "and certainly not if Your Majesty informs an ambassador directly on such decisive measures as possible mobilization without listening to me first. By virtue of the office with which Your Majesty has entrusted me, I bear responsibility for the policies Your Majesty orders before God and country, before history and my own conscience. Even Your Majesty cannot relieve me of this responsibility."

It was a manly avowal, and the Kaiser immediately retreated. Bethmann's letter points to a revealing distinction: he could reconcile himself more readily to a dangerous policy than to the imperial flouting of his authority. He would resign rather than accept both simultaneously. Bethmann's implicit distinction may help us to understand his complicated sense of the responsibility of power.

I have already suggested that he had a highly—in Imperial Germany, perhaps uniquely—developed sense of responsibility. He knew that future generations would hold him accountable for German policy, and his intelligence and realism made him recognize the potential dangers of that policy. He was cautious and circumspect and pondered the likely consequences of decisions. Often he appeared racked by doubts. Still, his sense of responsibility and his constant brooding did not paralyze him, as has sometimes been suggested. They may have given him the psychological reassurance for action. He stared before he leapt, but he leapt nevertheless.

Bethmann's sense of responsibility was attenuated by his political ideas and experiences and by certain personal beliefs. He sensed intuitively what Max Weber posited in his celebrated "Politics as Vocation" immediately after the war, that a politician "allows himself to come into contact with diabolical powers lurking in every form of violence." Bethmann probably would have agreed with a wartime observation by Riez-ler that "politics is really the art of doing evil and attaining the good—To be wise enough to know how everything is inter-locked [and] through malice to lead the ill-intentioned [*die bösen Willen*] to some-thing good." He appreciated the ambiguity of power, and the distinction between pri-vate and public morality.

He had, moreover, suffered from the fragmentation of power in Imperial Ger-many, and he understood the limits on its exercise. Hence the responsibility of power was parceled out as well. Bethmann bent to the decisions of others in authority, often assuaging his conscience by the correct assumption that if he were to resign, his opponents would follow a still more reckless course, aided by a Chancellor less conscien-tious than himself. He defended, as I have suggested, his office more stoutly than his policy. A sign of diffidence, perhaps, but of something deeper also. Max Weber's distinc-tion between the civil servant and politician is relevant: the politician's "conduct is sub-ject to quite a different, indeed, exactly the opposite, principle of responsibility from that of the civil servant. The honor of the civil servant is vested in his ability to execute conscientiously the order of superior author-ities, exactly as if the order agreed with his own conviction. This holds even if the order appears wrong to him and if, despite the civil servant's remonstrances, the authority insists on the order. Without this moral discipline and self-denial, in the highest sense, the whole apparatus would fall to pieces. The honor of the political leader, of the leading statesman, however, lies precisely in an exclusive *per-sonal* responsibility for what he does, a responsibility he cannot and must not reject or transfer." Bethmann's sense of responsi-bility, I think, was an uncertain mixture of these two types.

A further point must be considered: Bethmann was by temperament and perhaps conviction a pessimist. As the Great War drew closer, he seems to have become a fatalist as well. This foreknowledge of dis-aster probably eased his sense of responsi-bility and reinforced the feeling of resigned

duty that he had to stick to his job, however heavy the burden of decision, because a successor would be so much worse. In July 1914, his sense of responsibility, modified by these considerations, allowed him to take extreme risks and seek crafty subterfuges. For as the devoted but not uncritical Riezler wrote on July 7 and repeated later: "His cunning appears to be as great as his clumsi-ness." [*Seine Gerissenheit wohl ebenso gross wie sein Ungeschick.*]

The bulk of the Riezler diary pertains to the war itself, but the entries from July 7 to 23 offer unique insights into Bethmann's thoughts and conduct during the crisis weeks. They also record Riezler's gradual understanding of Bethmann's daring and complicated policy, designed to end what he thought was Germany's plight.

On July 6, the two men traveled to Hohenfinow together, and Riezler was struck by Bethmann's melancholy, attrib-uting it to his wife's death a few weeks before. That night, Riezler learned of the appalling dimensions of the crisis that had begun that morning with Germany's issuance of the "blank check" and her insistence that Austria honor it quickly and with aplomb. Bethmann told the unsuspecting Riezler "the secret news. . .which gives a shocking picture" of Germany's situation. Bethmann began with the Anglo-Russian negotiations for a naval convention and the prospect of a landing in Pomerania, "the last link in the chain." Russia was growing steadily stronger, Austria steadily weaker and incapable of ever fighting "as an ally in a German cause. The Entente knows that we are therefore entirely paralyzed."

The sequence of Bethmann's account makes it clear that his response to the murder of Sarajevo was determined by what he had long thought was Germany's precar-ious condition, not by the immediate effects of the assassination itself. Sarajevo unre-quited would worsen Germany's situation; Sarajevo properly exploited might lead to a dramatic escape from that situation.

On July 6, Bethmann spoke of "grave decisions." Official Serbia was implicated in the assassination, Austria sought to rouse herself, and Francis Joseph had asked the Emperor whether Germany considered the crisis as a *"casus foederis."* Bethmann added: "Our old dilemma with every Austrian action in the Balkans. If we encourage them, they say we pushed them into it; if we discourage them, they say we left them in the lurch. Then come the Western powers with open arms and we lose the last powerful ally." This remark seems in odd, but not atypical, contradiction to the fear that Austria was practically worthless as a German ally anyhow.

Bethmann warned that "an action against Serbia can lead to world war. The Chancellor expects that a war, whatever its outcome, will result in the uprooting of everything that exists. The existing [world] very antiquated, without ideas." He thought it was a symptom of the general blindness that conservatives hoped that a war would strengthen the monarchical order in Germany. "Thick fog over the people. The same in all of Europe. The future belongs to Russia. . . .The Chancellor very pessimistic about the intellectual condition of Germany."

What a strange mixture of motives and forebodings, of realism and pessimism! Yet this mixture constituted the background to Bethmann's decision to run the risk of war in July 1914.

On July 8, Bethmann added that if the war "comes from the east" and Germany goes to Austria's help and not the other way around, "then we shall have prospects for winning it. If the war does not come, if the Czar does not want it, or France, thoroughly bewildered, counsels peace, then we still have prospects of breaking up the Entente through this action." The Riezler diary sustains the view that Bethmann in early July had resolved on a forward course; by means of forceful diplomacy and a local Austrian war against Serbia he intended to detach England or Russia from the Entente or—if that failed—to risk a general war over an opportune issue at a still opportune moment.

But Bethmann realized the dangers of a military showdown. Already on July 14, he

correctly assessed the likely lineup of nations. "If in case of war, England starts at once, then Italy will under no circumstances come in." No wonder Riezler wrote on the same day: "Our situation is terrible."

On July 23, the Chancellor pointed out that if war came, it would come through precipitous Russian mobilization, before any negotiations. After mobilization, it would be too late for talks because the Germans would have to attack at once in order to have any chance of victory. "But then the whole people will feel the danger and will rise up." Bethmann envisioned the sequence of events that would lead up to a "defensive" war, provoked by Russia, which alone could unite the nation and perhaps even deceive other nations. Hence Bethmann was furious at the Crown Prince, who had sent bellicose messages to Pan-German groups. Such royal saber-rattling would obviously impair the credibility of this defensive war! In the same conversation he discussed the treatment of the socialists: in order to make sure of their support he would negotiate with them at once and in case of war forestall army action against them. Three days later, he was appalled at the recurrent idea of some generals to arrest all socialist leaders on the first day of war. The principal components of Bethmann's tactics for the outbreak and conduct of war appear here for the first time with remarkable clarity: the war must be defensive, the utterances of the Pan-German chauvinists subdued, and the socialists wooed. During the war, he discovered that these tactics proved his only possible strategy.

In a sense, the most damaging evidence that the Riezler diary provides for the July crisis lies in what it does *not* say: it contains no hint or thought of any move by Bethmann to arrest the crisis, to save the peace. Why, we must then ask, did Bethmann opt for and persist in this forward course that he recognized from the beginning was fraught with danger? Riezler confirms what we would suppose: he chose this course regretfully, broodingly. On July 14, he said that a war would destroy the familiar world and that it represented for him "a leap in the dark and [his] hardest duty." Time and again, during the war, he worried over his responsibility for leading Germany into it. The "defensive" character of war offered little solace to him.

Did it have to come to this? he asked on July 20. Should he have stuck to his resignation in 1912? But his successor— perhaps Tirpitz himself—would have been worse. Why was Germany in this predicament? "The earlier errors: simultaneously Turkish policy against Russia, Morocco against France, the navy against England— challenge everybody, put yourself in everybody's path, and actually weaken no one in this fashion. Reason: Aimlessness, the need for little prestige successes and solicitude for every current of public opinion. The 'national' parties which with their racket (*Radau*) about foreign policy want to preserve and strengthen their party position." A better analysis—or clearer indictment—of the fatality of Germany's prewar foreign policy could hardly have been made. It bears out completely a general observation that Riezler made in a prewar book: "The threat of war in our time lies. . .in the internal politics of those countries in which a weak government is confronted by a strong nationalist movement." Bethmann's judgment corresponds to Admiral von Müller's later view as to why the German government in July 1914 did not pursue a conciliatory policy: "The government, already weakened by domestic disunity, found itself inevitably under pressure from a great part of the German people which had been whipped into a high-grade chauvinism by Navalists [*Flottenvereinler*] and Pan-Germans."

Bethmann overcame or suspended his doubts. In fact, once he had resolved on this forward course, he shook off his habitual hesitancy. Already on July 20, Riezler noted that the mood was serious, "the Chancellor resolute and silent." A week later, he recorded that Bethmann "sees doom [*Fatum*] greater than human power hanging over Europe and our own people," but added on the same day, "he is entirely changed, has no time to brood, and is therefore fresh, active, and lively, without any disquiet." The juxta-position of fatalism and energy is not odd or unusual: Calvinists, too, believe in predestination and act decisively.

Obviously fatalism was a psychological condition, not a rational ground, for Bethmann's decision to run the risk of a world war. His fatalism went beyond the not uncommon assumption of the times that such a war was inevitable; he also believed that the world such a war would destroy was hopelessly superannuated, destined to be swept away. This, too, eased his sense of responsibility.

It has recently been suggested that Bethmann cherished expansionist aims, which he hoped to realize through war. Perhaps, but compelling evidence is lacking, and the Riezler diary offers no corroboration. Rather it suggests that his principal motive was fear for Germany's future. Bethmann's aims for the future were vague, his fears concrete, and the discrepancy allowed for the psychologically comforting half-truth that a war would be a defensive struggle. The diary does attest Bethmann's real terror at Russia's "growing demands and colossal explosive power." In a few years she would be supreme—and Germany her first, lonely victim.

In his dread of the future he seems never to have reckoned with the fluidity of the European political system or the likely workings of the balance of power. He feared the day when a thoroughly prepared Russia, supported by England, would crush Germany. But would England ever have supported the attack of a stronger Russia on a weaker Germany, thus establishing Russian hegemony in Europe? Or again: if Austria had in fact defected to the West, would not a return to a Russo-German alliance have offered a more than adequate counterweight? Bethmann barely considered these alternatives; in any case, he would not have persuaded the other rulers of Germany of their plausibility. Instead he remembered in those July days that Kiderlen-Wächter had always assumed the inevitability of war, and the implication was that Bethmann now at last accepted the dead man's judgment. Not that there was a dearth of living colleagues who urged him on.

Bethmann's anxiety about Germany's eventual isolation seems so exaggerated—as compared with even his own earlier estimates—that it may be legitimate to ask whether its intensity may in some small measure represent a kind of projection of his own melancholy stemming from his recent bereavement. His decision to risk war and his reluctance to do anything to save the peace was probably related to still another condition that combined personal and historical elements. For years he had been decried as a weakling. The military—but others too—frequently warned against another "Fashoda," which popular wisdom in those days, much like the indiscriminate warning against "Munich" today, adduced in order to preach a hard line against any compromise. Is it not likely that Bethmann's resolution in July 1914 was strengthened by a feeling that his policy of so-called conciliatoriness had yielded nothing, strengthened by the weariness of the civilian who had for so long been attacked by his tougher colleagues? It is a curious fact that in his postwar memoirs he defended his July course by arguing that the opposite course—accommodation of Russia—would have amounted to "self-castration" (*Selbstentmannung*)—an unconscious allusion perhaps to the frequent charges of civilian effeminacy? It is significant that two other principal actors of the July drama, Leopold Berchtold and Serge Sazonov, also smarted under their countrymen's allegations of earlier weakness. It is difficult to assess the importance, if any, of such often unconscious factors, but it seems arbitrary to ignore them altogether.

It is incontrovertible that Bethmann consciously risked a world war, but there is no evidence that he did so in order to establish German hegemony. It is naive and excessively rationalistic to suppose that aggression must spring from lust of conquest. Fear, too, impels aggressive action, and if the action succeeds, then, as Bethmann remarked in August 1914 about Moltke's war aims, *l'appétit vient en mangeant.*

Wolfgang Mommsen

WAR AS A PRODUCT OF GOVERNMENTAL INSTABILITY

Among German academic critics of Fritz Fischer none has been more thoughtful than Wolfgang Mommsen. Educated at Marburg, Köln, and the University of Leeds, Mommsen is currently professor of modern history at the University of Düsseldorf and has written extensively on modern imperialism. Initially, his criticisms of Fischer focused on both his approach and his conclusions, especially his treatment of Bethmann Hollweg. More recently Mommsen has subjected Fischer's examination of pre-1914 German politics to a rigorous, comparative assessment and

From Wolfgang Mommsen, "Domestic Factors in German Foreign Policy Before 1914," in *Central European History,* Vol. VI (March, 1973), pp. 11-12, 14-15, 21-22, 30-43. Used by permission of Wolfgang Mommsen and the editors of *Central European History.*

reached strikingly different conclusions about the motivation of Germany's foreign and domestic policy. He accepts Fischer's assertions that *Innenpolitik* in Germany was not stable and that this instability possibly contributed to decisions in July 1914. But Mommsen sees the policy decisions as far less calculated, far less cleverly or consistently planned, and much more the by-product of a government structure that had little steady direction. In sum, he retraces Fischer's contentions from an analytical or functional approach to reach a significantly different understanding of pre-1914 German politics.

THE ARGUMENTATION of Fritz Fischer appears to me to be much more important, and without doubt much more to the point. Whatever may be said about his opinions, he definitely deserves to be honored for having once more opened up the discussion of a vital issue which German historians had erroneously believed to be definitely settled. However, it remains to be seen whether his findings can also be considered the last word on German policy before 1914.

Fischer maintains that in the last analysis German foreign policy was the necessary outcome of an aggressive nationalism which pervaded almost all sections of German society and which, of course, was particularly strong among the ruling classes. In 1961 Fischer argued that Germany had been deliberately heading for a European war during the July crisis in 1914, in order to become a world power. Thereafter, step by step, he radicalized his position even more, eventually arriving at the thesis that Germany had decided upon going to war as early as 1911, or at any rate by December 8, 1912, in order to break out of the deadlock to which her previous attempts to acquire colonial territories and greater political influence overseas had led. He also maintained that the war aims Germany pursued after 1914 could be traced long before the war. He argued that this was particularly the case with regard to the acquisition of Longwy-Briey, but was also true with regard to the plan of establishing economic predominance on the European continent, possibly including the Balkans as well, by means of a Ger-

man-led European Economic Association. In his most recent book, *Der Krieg der Illusionen,* Fischer assembled enormous source material, partially derived from Wernecke's study on German public opinion before 1914, in order to substantiate his thesis.

It is not possible to present here a detailed critical analysis of Fischer's presentation of German politics between 1911 and 1915. Yet it seems obvious that he has been driven too far regarding his main thesis: Germany's "will to power." It may be said, for instance, that Fischer is not at all clear as to the question of which sections and groups of German society really advocated a policy of war in order to cut at one stroke the Gordian knot of German imperialism. Was it the government, the emperor, the military establishment, the Conservatives, the industrialists, or the nation at large, any one of them, or all of them? Actually Fischer's arguments constantly shift, charging at times one group, at times another with warlike tendencies; but they are never consistent in this respect. And he does not claim that the various groups and persons with which he is dealing were all, and at all times, committed to going to war. Although at many points we gain important new insights into what was going on, his overall thesis is far from clear. . . .

It is also open to some doubt whether German imperialism had really come to a dead end by 1914, as is gloomily argued over and over again by Fischer. Germany's economic position in the Ottoman Empire had been consolidated, although this had necessitated some concessions both to French and British interests in this sphere. But it had *not* been diminished, even given the chronic problem of the relative scarcity of capital for "political" investments overseas.

It would appear that the very nature of Fischer's approach makes it difficult for him to give proper consideration to the forces of moderation. He draws his conclusions rather from what people said than from what they actually did. Thus, the aggressive nationalist outburst of the politicians concerned are often taken as the whole of the story. On the other hand, it must be admitted that Fischer makes a serious attempt to get beyond an interpretation dealing mainly with ideological aspects, at least in his "second" book, although not always with the same degree of success. Nonetheless, it seems warranted to conclude that he arrives at all too radical conclusions, mainly because he tends to isolate quotations of a nationalist or imperialist nature from the context, and bases his conclusions on those quotations rather than on a coherent analysis of the political and social structures.

There is still another point worth mentioning. The premise of Fischer's interpretation of Wilhelmine politics, that an aggressive nationalism lay at the bottom of all that happened, induces him to describe the actions of other powers as mere reactions prompted by German diplomacy itself. Yet neither French nationalism nor the growing militarist tendencies in Russia can be properly explained in such a way. A comparative study of European nationalism would reveal that the gradually growing participation of the masses of the population in the political process was everywhere accompanied by an intensified nationalism. . . .

If, at the turn of the century, Bülow had succeeded in preventing an open conflict with the Reichstag by playing the imperialist tune, Bethmann Hollweg decided not to embark upon such a frivolous policy—with one notable exception with which we shall soon have to deal. He believed that the political situation after the crisis of 1909 was not a propitious moment for an adventurous foreign policy, and that time would

be required to let things calm down again at home. Bethmann Hollweg's primary concern in the years from 1909 to 1911 was the stabilization of the position of the German Empire within the system of powers. Germany backed out of the somewhat odd position on Morocco which she had assumed at Algeciras, in spite of the noise the Mannesmann Brothers made on behalf of it. The government also tried to bring about a détente with Russia, an undertaking which initially appeared to have worked quite successfully. Otherwise, Bethmann Hollweg worked hard to improve relations with Great Britain, even after a not very sensible attempt to negotiate a neutrality agreement in return for a moderate limitation of naval construction had failed. . . .

The chancellor believed that the only way out was to conduct foreign policy in almost absolute secrecy, holding back from the public at large, and even from the party leaders, all but the most elementary information. Bethmann Hollweg was fully aware that by doing this he exposed himself to vicious attacks from Conservatives and extreme nationalists alike, as his policy inevitably appeared to outsiders inconsistent and weak. In spite of this unfortunate fact, he refused to put forward any specific program. He did not act upon suggestions by Rathenau to give the country a lead in matters of foreign policy, being convinced that publicity was bound to impair the chances of ultimate success. Riezler wrote at the time, not without some conceit, that only a foreign policy which did *not* care for the applause of the public, and which was *not* heading for quick results, was likely to achieve anything worthwhile.

To put things another way: Bethmann Hollweg never tried and consequently never succeeded in selling his policy to the country at large, and for this reason he was largely at the mercy of the various groupings within the ruling elite. For the time being his political concept was accepted by the emperor and, though not without some misgivings, by the military establishment and the conservative bureaucracy. This was all the more true because Bethmann Hollweg had reluctantly given in to the requests of the navy as well as the General Staff by increasing both the army and the navy in 1912, and by putting through parliament another considerable increase of the army in 1913. A strong army was, up to a point, in line with his political concept, for he considered the strong, unassailable position of the German Empire on the European continent as the fundamental prerequisite for an expansive foreign policy elsewhere. On the other hand, he sincerely believed that an improvement in Anglo-German relations would be the key to a solution of the difficult problems German diplomacy was facing. Better relations with Great Britain would serve two purposes. First, they would reduce the danger of a European conflagration, and this would enable Germany to steer somewhat more confidently through the troubled waters ahead, with a crisis-ridden Austria-Hungary as ally and a rapidly rising Russia as a possible enemy. Second, there was reasonable hope that Germany could secure some of her colonial objectives with British assistance, in particular in Central Africa, but also in the Near East and perhaps even in China.

Bethmann Hollweg could reckon at least to some degree on the support of the National Liberal and Center parties, although the Anglophobia prevailing there was difficult to overcome. Furthermore, he was able to establish fairly intimate relations with some of the major banking houses; they could be induced, up to a point, to invest in the spheres of interest the government attempted to peg out in Africa and elsewhere in rather sophisticated diplomatic negotiations—even though the prospects for returns on such investments were gloomy indeed, apart from the fact that capital was scarce anyway. Relations with big industry, however, were by no means good; and many of the industrialists were not at all interested in a German Central Africa. Their interests were more in the Near East, so far as they had any definite interests at all. Some people, such as Rathenau, came around to the idea that it might be more useful to concentrate economic activities on the Euro-

pean continent, rather than pegging out claims for posterity overseas. Bethmann Hollweg did his best to set the stage for a continuation of German economic penetration of the Ottoman Empire, though he took care to let the British have a share in this too. But it was only under the pressure of war that he joined the camp of the advocates of a European Economic Association dominated by Germany, as an alternative to old-fashioned territorial imperialism.

There can be no doubt that the government of Bethmann Hollweg did not seriously contemplate attaining any of its objectives by war until May—June 1914—with the possible exception of a liquidation of the Ottoman Empire taking place without the Germans getting a proper share. Bethmann Hollweg was confident that he could get along without a war, although by the end of 1913 he became increasingly worried about the deteriorating position of the German Empire within the European system of powers. He stuck to a peaceful policy, all the more so because he was convinced that the existing political order probably would not survive a war. Fritz Fischer has argued again and again that Bethmann Hollweg's repeated attempts to negotiate a neutrality agreement with Great Britain were part and parcel of a policy of expansion by means of war. Britain should be made to stand aside in order to allow Germany safely to crush France and Russia—this, he maintains, was the core of German calculations. This is, however, not borne out by the sources. It will have to be admitted that a neutrality agreement—or something coming fairly close to it—played, so to speak, a token role in the internal struggle between Tirpitz and William II on one side, and Bethmann Hollweg and the Foreign Office on the other. This state of affairs existed behind the scenes during and after the visit of Lord Haldane to Berlin in February 1912. The group in favor of a hard line was not willing to make substantial sacrifices in naval construction unless the British would indicate that they were willing to change substantially their allegedly unfriendly attitude toward Germany. The inconsistent attitude of the German Foreign

Office during February and March 1912 with regard to how much should be asked from the British government in return for a naval agreement cannot be explained except as a reflection of the ups and downs of the internal struggle going on in Berlin.

Bethmann Hollweg was unable at this time to carry out his policy. However, the failure of the Anglo-German negotiations in 1912 did not discourage him. He still thought that an improvement of relations with Britain, accompanied by colonial concessions, was within reach. Naturally, he came to be considered inside the ruling elite as an essentially pro-British statesman, and his political fortunes came to be tied up with the development of Anglo-German relations. Early in December 1912 Sir Edward Grey conveyed to the German government an explicit warning that in case of a European war developing from the Balkan crisis, Great Britain would come to the assistance of France and Russia. In court circles this was considered positive proof that Bethmann Hollweg's expectations as regards Great Britain were unfounded (which, as a matter of fact, was not the case), and as mentioned already the emperor at once consulted Tirpitz and the military leaders, behind the back of the "civilians," as to how to prepare the country for the European war which in his opinion seemed imminent. Bethmann Hollweg's prestige was at a low ebb. Although the chancellor soon regained ground, he henceforth was aware how unstable his position had become.

It must be realized, moreover, that since 1913 Bethmann Hollweg's moderate course had been challenged increasingly by a considerable section of the ruling elite, in particular by the General Staff. And, as has been shown above, the latter's influence had risen substantially. The military leaders were seriously worried about the reappearance of Russia as a first-rate military power, and—as we know now beyond doubt—they were harboring the idea of a preventive war against Russia and France, for within a few years the Schlieffen Plan would no longer work. Moltke, so far as we can see from the scattered sources, became increasingly annoyed with the diplomats, who kept saying that since relations with Great Britain were improving the dangerous period ahead could be overcome. It is possible that the article of an *Oberleutnant* Ulrich published in March 1914 in the *Kölnische Zeitung,* which brought about a heated press controversy between German and Russian newspapers, had been initiated by somebody close to the German General Staff; although any proof for this is lacking, it seems possible, since this article expressed the fears and apprehensions in German military quarters rather precisely.

It is at this point that pressure from the public at large also has to be given proper attention. The relations among the military establishment, the court, and the Conservatives were, of course, fairly intimate. In conservative quarters, as well as in the Pan-German League, the assumption was indeed widely held that a war was likely to have a healthy effect on German national character. Furthermore, a war appeared to be convenient in order to set the clock in the interior "right" again.

It goes without saying that this is only a part of the story. For the belief that the diplomatic situation had deteriorated alarmingly in the last years, and that a European war was imminent, had spread to a considerable proportion of the middle classes too. The warlike message of Friedrich Bernhardi's *Germany and the Next War,* which was couched in a language that may be called a peculiar mixture of the bourgeois cultural heritage and militant nationalism, did not fail to have some impact on the German intelligentsia. Yet the pressure exerted on the government by important sections of German society in favor of a tough line in matters of foreign policy does not suffice to explain the course of events which eventually led to the outbreak of the First World War. The popularity of imperialism accounts for much of what happened, but there is no evidence that specific influences of this kind played a major role in the deliberations of the German government on the eve of the war. It was, rather, the crisis of the governmental system as such which induced the men at the top to take refuge in an aggressive political strategy.

It has been pointed out already that the government of Bethmann Hollweg could not count on the support of any of the major political groupings in the Reichstag or in the country at large. For this very reason it was more dependent than any government since Bismarck on the goodwill of the conservative establishment, and in particular the entourage of William II, which was connected with the former through a great many social connections. Since 1913 the Conservatives had launched a series of vitriolic attacks against the chancellor, and had tried to convince the emperor that he was neither tough enough with the Social Democrats nor effective in holding the Reichstag parties in check. The Pan-German League hoped to exploit this situation. In October 1913 Class attempted to bring about the fall of the chancellor; with the assistance of the Crown Prince, a long memorandum in which General von Gebsattel assailed the supposedly weak foreign policy of the chancellor was brought to the attention of the emperor. Although William II was not yet prepared to dismiss his chancellor, the position of Bethmann Hollweg was precarious indeed, and he had to fear the charge that his foreign policy was both weak and ineffective.

By far the most serious challenge to Bethmann Hollweg's foreign policy came, however, from the General Staff. The military leaders were extremely concerned about the prospect that the main premise of the Schlieffen Plan, namely, a slow Russian mobilization which would allow the German army to crush France before the Russians became an effective military danger, was being undermined by the progress of Russian armaments, and in particular by the completion of the railways in western Russia. Their apprehensions were not reduced by the rather ambiguous official Russian reaction to press charges that Russia was preparing a war against Germany. In May or June 1914 Moltke therefore suggested that the government ought to bring about a war, while Germany was still in a position to win it. Obviously, the idea of a preventive war

was gaining ground in governmental quarters. Even William II, who despite all his militaristic pathos was essentially in favor of peace, was in doubt as to whether it might not be wiser to take up arms before the Russian armament program was completed, as he confided to Warburg in June 1914.

Outside the inner circle of the government other considerations also came into play. Quite a few people, such as Heydebrandt und der Lasa, maintained that a war would be a splendid opportunity to smash the Social Democrats. Bethmann Hollweg was furious about such "nonsense," presumably because he was aware of the consequences for his political position if such views were taken up by the emperor. Bethmann Hollweg emphatically denied that a European war would strengthen the case of the conservatives. Rather, it was likely to benefit the Social Democrats; it might even result in the dethronement of some monarchs. The somewhat scanty sources do not allow all too radical conclusions; yet it can be gathered from them that Bethmann Hollweg and Jagow apparently had a difficult time fending off such ideas. They were careful to make clear that they were not, in principle, against the idea of a preventive war—any other stand might have been interpreted as weakness—yet they nonetheless took exception to the suggestion of solving the problems of German diplomacy by a preventive war. Their main argument was that in view of the improving relations with Great Britain it would be folly to pursue such a policy.

The strength of the position of the chancellor within the complicated governmental system of Wilhelmine Germany depended to a very large degree on his status as responsible leader of foreign policy. William II did not like the idea of changing the chancellor primarily because he feared the repercussions in diplomatic relations. In this respect, the fairly positive image which Bethmann Hollweg enjoyed in Great Britain was of great importance. Under such conditions the news about a forthcoming Anglo-Russian naval agreement—which had reached Berlin in May 1914 through a spy in the

British Embassy in Saint Petersburg—had a disastrous effect on the domestic position of the chancellor. And just as in December 1912, the protagonists of a "forward policy" again got the upper hand. Bethmann Hollweg's main argument against a preventive war, namely, that the British government would help in preventing the Russians from going to war, had gone to pieces overnight. Even worse, the British seemed to be about to join forces once and for all with the Russians and the French; and this played into the hands of those who argued that since the military situation of the German Empire was getting worse and worse it would be better to fight the assumedly "inevitable" war as soon as possible. This situation is rather frankly alluded to in Bethmann Hollweg's message to Lichnowsky for Sir Edward Grey of June 16, 1914.

Bethmann Hollweg was well known for his essentially pro-British orientation. Therefore, the sudden collapse of his hope that a rapprochement with Great Britain was within reach was grist to the mills of his domestic foes. For this reason Bethmann Hollweg was not very outspoken about his own estimate of the British attitude toward Germany in the event of a European war. It is worth noting that the chancellor did not reckon with British neutrality in a European war, although this was believed by many people at the time (and subsequently by many historians). In his opinion, more intimate relations between the German Empire and Great Britain would help to stabilize the German position on the Continent, and reduce the danger of a European conflagration over a new Balkan crisis. Furthermore, it would ease German economic and political expansion overseas. Bethmann Hollweg was, however, well aware that the British would never allow Germany to crush France while standing aside themselves. The most the chancellor expected was that Great Britain might remain neutral in the initial phase of a European war, while trying to bring about a diplomatic solution. In 1914 he counted on British help in avoiding a European war, but not on British neutrality, all the more so because all available information pointed to

the contrary. The assumption that Great Britain might remain neutral did not play a key role in German calculations on the eve of the First World War. Rather, the opposite is true. It was the startling news that Great Britain was apparently about to join the opposite camp that set things in motion. It added additional strength to the argument of the domestic rivals of the chancellor that it might be wiser to forestall the formation of a more definite entente, which would encourage Russia to go ahead with warlike measures, by launching a preventive war as soon as a convenient opportunity was at hand.

This is borne out by the course of events which culminated in the decision of Germany to let the Austrians and Hungarians have their punitive war against Serbia, whatever the eventual outcome might be, although the government was well aware that an Austro-Serbian conflict could easily escalate into a European war. Up to then German diplomacy had pursued a relatively pro-Serbian course; several times it had prevented the Austrians from interfering by force in the conflicts of the Balkan states. To the dismay of the Austrians, Berchtold had been told over and over again that it might after all be best to come to terms with Serbia in some way or other. In the first days after Francis Ferdinand's assassination the *Wilhelmstrasse* seems to have stuck to its previous line. This was indicated by the attitude of the Russophobe Tschirschky, to which early in July the emperor took violent exception. The decision to give Austria-Hungary a sort of "blank check" was a major shift in German policy, and it is reported that Bethmann Hollweg agreed to it only after some hesitation. In principle this decision was reached *before* Count Hoyos arrived in Berlin on July 5—presumably around the 2nd or 3rd. This decision amounted to a sort of compromise between the position to which the chancellor and the Foreign Office had adhered hitherto and the General Staff's position that Germany should not work for peace if there was an opportunity to have right now the big showdown with Russia and France which they assumed would come anyway within the next few years. Bethmann Hollweg himself admitted (as he confessed later) that, provided that the generals' estimate of the situation of the Central Powers and the warlike tendencies of Tsarist Russia was correct, it might indeed be better to have the war at once rather than later. Consequently, Bethmann Hollweg embarked upon a "diagonal" course, that is, to let Austria act as an "agent provocateur," and make the Serbian war a test case regarding the question of whether Russia was bent on war anyway, or not. In doing so he satisfied the request of the military establishment that Germany should *not* avoid a war, if it was in the offing, without fully endorsing their strategy, which was bent on a preventive war. He assumed that Russia was not ready for war, and that there was a genuine chance of breaking the ring of the Entente powers without a European war. Although all persons involved in this decision were fully aware of the fact that a Serbian action by Austria-Hungary could provoke a European war—in which case the chancellor expected Russia to begin the war within days—he and the Foreign Office, at least, assumed that the Russians would back down, all the more so since neither France nor Great Britain was enthusiastic about going to war on behalf of Serbia. It may be pointed out that a declaration of the British government to the effect that Great Britain would not remain neutral would not have altered the course of events a bit. On the contrary, it would have been grist to the mills of Moltke, and would have amounted to a further strengthening of his argument that in view of the steadily deteriorating position of the German Empire it was better to fight now, at a moment when in his opinion the war could still be won decisively within months, rather than later.

The political calculation of the German government amounted to gambling with very high stakes indeed. Bethmann Hollweg himself called it "a leap in the dark" which was dictated by "most severe duty." The chancellor's position was no longer strong enough to get any alternative accepted by the inner ring of the ruling elite. His plan was a fairly precise reflection of the deep division within the government itself. It was a compromise between two rival schemes. It did not directly work for war; rather, it favored a diplomatic solution of the crisis. Still, it satisfied the request of the military establishment insofar as it did nothing to avoid war. The attempt to maneuver Russia into a position in which *she* would have to decide about peace or war was not dictated only by the consideration that otherwise the Social Democrats might not rally behind the government. It was equally influenced by the calculation that only in this way could the forthcoming crisis be exploited diplomatically, and with the afterthought that, provided the Russians shrank back from extreme measures, the fears of the German General Staff could be positively disproved.

Hence, it was not so much lust for world power as weakness and confusion which induced Bethmann Hollweg to embark upon such a political strategy. The contradictions which can be discovered in the calculations of the German government in July 1914 are a rather precise reflection of the sharp antagonisms within the German ruling elite. It must be added, however, that this was possible only because those groups which were part of this elite (namely, the upper stratum of the governmental bureaucracy, the General Staff and behind it the officer corps, and the conservative entourage of the emperor) enjoyed a political influence which was out of proportion to their actual importance in German society as a whole. This was partly due to the fact that the stalemate on the level of parliamentary politics had enabled the government to carry on with its policies as if nothing had happened at all. It is noteworthy that the government could afford to disregard entirely the opinions of the party leaders in July 1914. Indeed, there is no evidence that any of the party leaders was given the opportunity to have a say in the decisions of the government. The chancellor seems to have been confident that at least the bourgeois parties, with the possible exception of the Progressives, would support a bold course in preference to a policy which would pass over the opportunity of Sarajevo without any attempt to come to Austria-Hungary's assistance, and to exploit the crisis to the advantage of the Central Powers.

It is doubtful whether Bethmann Hollweg, even if he had cared to consult the party leaders, would have found among the bourgeois parties wholehearted support against the champions of a preventive war. But surely the party leaders would not have agreed to a crisis strategy which was so designed as to please both the hawks and the doves, and which for this very reason was bound to fail. This is, of course, a rather speculative argument. Yet one point can safely be made, namely, that the desperate attempts of the government of Bethmann Hollweg to prevent any substantial constitutional change in the face of a more or less hostile Reichstag made it extremely dependent on the goodwill of those small groups within the German upper class which favored a policy of suppression in the interior just as much as a tough line in foreign politics.

In the last analysis, we may conclude, the causes of the First World War must be sought not in the blunders and miscalculations of the governments alone, but in the fact that Germany's governmental system, as well as Austria-Hungary's and Russia's, was no longer adequate in the face of rapid social change and the steady advance of mass politics.

James Joll

THE INTELLECTUAL MILIEU AS AN EXPLANATION: THE UNSPOKEN ASSUMPTIONS

Few historians outside Germany have participated more actively in the discussion of Fritz Fischer's views than the distinguished British historian, James Joll. Not only did he write the introduction to the English translation of Fischer's *Germany's Aims in the First World War,* but he also wrote articles that sought to place Fischer's interpretation within the larger canvas of both German and international history. In his articles Joll's interest in intellectual history and his comparative approach ensured Fischer's work would be assessed in a larger context. Author of *Three Intellectuals in Politics* and the popular *Europe Since 1870* among other works, Joll has consistently urged that discussions about the start of World War I be viewed from a multi-dimensional and not wholly national standpoint.

Not surprisingly, therefore, in his inaugural lecture as Stevenson Professor of International Relations at the University of London in 1968,

From James Joll, "1914: The Unspoken Assumptions," in *The Origins of the First World War: Great Power Rivalry and German War Aims,* ed. H. W. Koch (New York: Taplinger Publishing Co., 1972), pp. 307-328. © 1972 by H. W. Koch. Reprinted by permission of Taplinger Publishing Company and of Macmillan, London and Basingstoke.

Joll addressed the issue of 1914 from an intellectual and comparative perspective. He did not ignore the contributions of diplomatic historians, but he argued that diplomatic history ought also to examine the "unspoken assumptions" held by statesmen and seek to understand the intellectual and cultural milieu in which they functioned. His admonitions, sparked by Fischer and yet no mere echo, form a veritable agenda for historians.

T HE CRISIS of July 1914 is probably better documented than any other in modern history, and because of the political implications of the question of "war guilt" and the explicit references in the Treaty of Versailles to Germany's responsibility for the war, the literature on the subject, both academic and polemical, is vast. Historians at least have reason to be grateful to the authors of the "war-guilt" clause in the Treaty, since it prompted the publication of the documents and the opening of the archives. There are admittedly some people who belittle the importance of the First World War and who believe that it will seem to future historians just the first round of a comparatively unimportant European civil war when set against the perspective of the changes in Africa, Asia and America during the twentieth century, and there are others who point out that the economic and social changes resulting from the war would have happened in any case, and that the war merely brought about a small acceleration of the pace at which they occurred. Still, for most of us the First World War and its origins remain topics of interest and relevance, while the recent controversy in Germany aroused by the publication of Professor Fritz Fischer's work on Germany's war aims shows that the subject is still one which can arouse deep political passions.

Why does this interest persist, in spite of the fact that there is little more we can hope to obtain in the way of documentary evidence—though it would be interesting to have some more information about exactly what passed between the French President and Prime Minister and their Russian colleagues during their visit to St. Petersburg from 20 to 24 July? Why do we still study the coming of the First World War, even though every incident in the critical days of July 1914 has been scrutinised, analysed and interpreted again and again? One of the answers lies, I think, in the discrepancy between the importance of the events themselves and of their consequences and the ordinariness of most of the politicians and generals making the key decisions. Luigi Albertini, himself a practising politician and newspaper editor, whose three vast volumes on the origins of the war still, in my opinion, remain the best of the detailed studies, wrote of "the disproportion between their intellectual and moral endowments and the gravity of the problems which faced them, between their acts and the results thereof." And Gavrilo Princip himself, whose assassination of the Archduke Franz Ferdinand on 28 June 1914 must in some sense be counted as one of the causes of the war, when asked by Dr. Pappenheim, the psychiatrist who interviewed him in prison, whether he believed the assassination was a service, replied that "he could not believe that the world war was a consequence of the assassination; that he could not feel himself responsible for the catastrophe and therefore could not say if it was a service, but he feared he did it in vain." Again and again in the July crisis one is confronted with men who suddenly feel themselves trapped, caught up in a fate they are unable to control. Bethmann Hollweg, the German Chancellor, for example, is reported as saying on 20 July 1914 that he saw "a doom (*ein Fatum*) greater than human power hanging over Europe and our own people." In some cases this sense of helplessness is because the politicians' gambles have gone wrong. In others, lack of understanding of the technical aspects of war led to the taking of military measures which turned out to be irreversible. "It will run away with him, as it ran away with me," the Kaiser said about Hitler to an English visitor to Doorn in the 1930s. Did he perhaps have in mind that moment on the afternoon of 1 August 1914 when, in a last-minute attempt to limit the war, he asked his military leaders whether it would not be possible to give up the idea of attacking France and to concentrate the German armies against Russia, only to be told to his annoyance that it was out of the question to undo the plans elaborated over many years, and that instead of an army ready for war he would have a mass of armed men with no food.

When political leaders are faced with the necessity of taking decisions the outcome of which they cannot foresee, in crises which they do not wholly understand, they fall back on their own instinctive reactions, traditions and modes of behaviour. Each of them has certain beliefs, rules or objectives which are taken for granted; and one of the limitations of documentary evidence is that few people bother to write down, especially in moments of crisis, things which they take for granted. Yet if we are to understand their motives, we must somehow try to find out what, as we say, "goes without saying." Even when we have records of what was said, we do not always know the tone of voice in which the words were spoken. What was the inflection with which the Russian Foreign Minister, Sazonov, exclaimed on hearing of the terms of the Austrian ultimatum to Serbia, *"C'est la guerre européenne?"* Or what were the overtones in the voice of the old Emperor Franz Josef when he greeted the report of the Serbian rejection of Austria-Hungary's terms with the untranslatable *"Also, doch!"*? Did the speakers express pain, regret, relief or surprise? Our judgment of their policies depends in part on the answer; and our answers depend on the picture of their character built up from a number of other sources, so that although we can be certain of the words they used, our interpretation may vary according to our assessment of quite different evidence about their characters.

In moments of crisis, political leaders fall back on unspoken assumptions, and their intentions can often only be judged in the light of what we can discover about those assumptions. It is this that makes it possible for the same document to serve as a basis for totally different interpretations. Let me give an example arising out of Professor Fritz Fischer's work on German war aims and the outbreak of war in 1914. Professor Fischer found in the archives, and published, a memorandum prepared for the German Chancellor dated 9 September 1914. It is a statement of war aims drawn up at a moment when the effects of the Battle of the Marne were not yet clear and when, therefore, the Germans still had good grounds for expecting a quick victory in the West. This programme is a comprehensive scheme for annexations in France and Belgium and for the establishment of German hegemony in central Europe through the creation of a Mitteleuropa under German leadership. The September Memorandum has strong similarities with a document sent to the Chancellor a few days earlier by the industrialist and financier, Walter Rathenau, the head of the great electricity combine, the A.E.G. We know that Bethmann-Hollweg and Rathenau were neighbours in the country and that they dined together from time to time. What did they talk about on these evenings? Were German gains in a possible war already being discussed before August 1914 around the table in Rathenau's exquisite dining room in Schloss Freienwalde? If so, how far were these aims in the minds of the German leaders in the critical days of July 1914? It is extremely hard to say; and our assessment of the significance of the September Memorandum of war aims depends on our general view of the mentality, the *Weltanschauung*, of the German leaders as much as on the document itself. Some historians regard the September Memorandum as a hastily contrived plan to meet the immediate situation when Germany was confronted with the prospect of an early and unexpected victory. Others maintain that it is evidence of the sinister nature of Germany's pre-war policies and of the views of what we would today call the military-industrial complex which controlled the German government. The links between the general ideas in the air before the war started and the concrete programme produced once war had begun are not in the document but in the minds of Germany's rulers; and it is on one's reconstruction of what was in their minds that our judgment of their actions must be based.

How can historians set about reconstructing the unspoken assumptions of the men they are studying? It is at this point that we look hopefully for assistance from other disciplines and turn to the psychologists or the sociologists or the economists. However, the help they can give us is limited. Either what they have to say is too general to fit a particular individual or a particular situation or—as in the attempts which have been made to use the techniques of psychoanalysis in dealing with historical characters—the type of evidence available is too fragmentary to provide the basis for more than very tentative or rather obvious hypotheses. Even Ambassador Bullitt's enlistment of the help of Freud in person for his study of Woodrow Wilson, although it produced a more interesting book than is generally allowed and gave Freud the chance of writing an excellent summary of some of his ideas, throws more light on Woodrow Wilson's personal relationships and on the psychological causes of his physical collapse than it does on his actual policies. Yet there are occasional hints which deserve following up and flashes of evidence which the amateur psychologist in each of us cannot help seizing on. Professor Fritz Stern, for example, has recently drawn attention to the fact that Bethmann-Hollweg in his memoirs wrote that for Germany to have followed a different course in July 1914 would have amounted to *Selbstent mannung*—self-castration—and suggests that the phrase might be an unconscious allusion to the charges of civilian effeminacy levelled by the soldiers at the politicians in Germany.

The historian must seek his explanations where he can find them, even in unorthodox or unprofessional places. After all, even L. B. Namier was not ashamed to use the services of a graphologist in reconstructing the character of the writer of manuscript documents. In general, however, other disciplines in the social sciences can usually only suggest new types of explanation and direct attention to new areas where the answers may lie. They cannot, that is to say, themselves provide the precise answers to the historians' questions. To take the most famous and obvious example, Marx, by drawing attention to the way in which economic factors produce historical change, has had an immensely fruitful influence on historical writing. Yet, when one comes to trace the exact effect of economic factors in, for instance, the crisis of 1914, one is faced with all sorts of puzzles. If, as I suggested earlier, some of the German industrialists and bankers were dreaming of a German economic sphere in central Europe and possibly envisaging a war as a means of achieving this, other economic leaders were pressing in a different direction. Take the case of Morocco, for example—an important element in the international tension before 1914. Here it was the French government which had had to persuade the bankers to lend money to the Sultan in order to support French political aims, and not the bankers who were pressing for political action to further their economic interests; and German policy in Morocco between 1909 and 1911 can only be understood when one realises that the German government and one group of mining interests wanted to co-operate with France, while a rival German group was trying to break this co-operation in their own interests. In the July crisis of 1914, while some industrialists may have looked forward to war as an opportunity of extending their influence and increasing their profits, many of the financiers and bankers were appalled at the economic chaos which they expected from war. In London, Grey was still, on 31 July, worried about the financial consequences of being involved in war. "The commercial and financial situation was extremely serious," he told the French Ambassador, "there was danger of a complete collapse that would involve us and everyone in ruin; and it was possible that our standing aside might be the only means of preventing a complete collapse of European credit in which we should be involved." And, again on 31 July, the old Lord Rothschild sent for the financial editor of *The Times* to try and stop the paper advocating intervention on the side of France and Russia, a suggestion indignantly refused by its recipient, who returned to his office white with rage.

Clearly it is extremely important to look at the economic pressures on the governments of Europe in the crisis of 1914, but the pressures will not turn out to have been all in one direction, and no economic explanation will give us the whole reason for the decisions taken. It is certainly true that the financiers and industrialists exercised great influence on the governments of Europe before 1914, but it is not true that the interests of the various economic pressure groups coincided, except that they seem to have agreed in expecting the war to be a short one. This means that it is very hard to determine at any particular moment which of the economic pressure groups was having a decisive influence on the decisions of a particular politician.

General economic or sociological explanations are important in providing us with a broad sense of what is happening in history. It is only rarely that they can give us the precise link between the general and the particular which we need to account for the individual event the historian is trying to explain. The same difficulty confronts us when we try to relate the general climate of ideas and the general ideological background of the time to the particular actions of the politicians and generals who brought Europe into war in 1914. However, I want to suggest one or two areas where we might start to look for clues to help us to reconstruct the unspoken presuppositions of the participants in the drama of 1914. Let us take the case of one of the leading characters, the British Foreign Secretary, Sir Edward Grey. As Foreign Secretary in a Liberal government,

most of whose members were more interested in domestic reform than in international affairs, Grey had borne much of the responsibility for the development of British foreign policy between 1905 and 1914. He has been accused both of pursuing a deliberate policy of isolating and encircling Germany and at the same time of contributing to the German decision to go to war in 1914 by hesitating to declare British support for France and Russia in time to deter Germany. I do not think either of these charges is justified, but it is true that Grey was a puzzling mixture of political shrewdness and political naiveté. At times his views on international affairs were of a surprising simplicity: "It is in German diplomacy alone," he wrote to President Theodore Roosevelt in 1906, "that one now meets with deliberate attempts to make mischief between other countries by saying poisoned things to one about the other." And there are many other examples of his regarding relations between States as being comparable to those between individuals, to be conducted on the same basis and the same principles as those between English country gentlemen.

Sir Charles Webster, in his Inaugural Lecture in the Stevenson Chair, called on historians to study the implications of the term "guarantee" in international relations and pointed out the importance of discovering "what exactly had been in the minds of statesmen when they undertook such obligations on behalf of their country." In the case of Grey, it often seems as though it was a simple schoolboy sense of honour which was the criterion by which he judged his own and other people's political actions. He had already expressed his dilemma clearly in February 1906, when a war between France and Germany over Morocco seemed a possibility. "If there is war between France and Germany," he wrote, "it will be very difficult for us to keep out of it. The *Entente* and still more the constant and emphatic demonstrations of affection (official, naval, political, commercial, municipal and in the Press) have created in France a belief that we shall support them in war. . . .If this expectation is disappointed, the French will never forgive us. There would also I think be a general feeling that we had behaved badly and left France in the lurch. . . .As a minor matter the position of any Foreign Secretary here, who had made it an object to maintain the *entente* with France, would become intolerable. On the other hand the prospect of a European War and of our being involved in it is horrible."

In 1914 Grey was thinking in the same terms, and was constantly remembering his exchange of letters with the French Ambassador in 1912, in which he had written: "I agree that, if either government had grave reason to expect an unprovoked attack by a third Power, or something that threatened the general peace, it should immediately discuss with the other, whether both Governments should act together to prevent aggression and to preserve peace, and if so what measures they would be prepared to take in common. If these measures involved action, the plans of the General Staffs would at once be taken into consideration, and the Governments would then decide what effect should be given to them." Although Grey had for political reasons to point out that this exchange did not necessarily commit the British government to action, for him there seems no doubt that it was a moral commitment; and it was agonising for him in July 1914 to realise that other members of the government and the Liberal Party did not see things in the same light, and that, while Paul Cambon, the French Ambassador, was playing on the British sense of fair play and asking if the word "honour" was to be crossed out of the English dictionary, the *Manchester Guardian* was complaining that: "By some hidden contract England has been technically committed behind her back to the ruinous madness of a share in the violent gamble of a war between two militarist leagues on the Continent."

All I am trying to say is that it would be a mistake to interpret Grey's policies in too subtle or sophisticated a way or to attribute to him too many long-term deep purposes. His unspoken premises remained the ethical code of a high-principled, slightly priggish

Wykehamist, and it is to his school days that we must look for a key to his fundamental attitudes. As he himself wrote later of his boyhood at school at Winchester: "I was becoming a 'Wykehamist.' All that is conveyed by this word can be understood by people who are Wykehamists. The ways of the place, its traditions and the country in which it is set were all getting a hold upon my heart. I had gained something which had become an inseparable part of my affection, which was part of my life's unalterable good. . . ." It is to his education and the education of the class to which he belonged that we must look for the key to much of Grey's later political behaviour; and this suggests that we should in general pay more attention to the links between educational systems and foreign policy, between the values and beliefs inculcated at school and the presuppositions on which politicians act later in life. In Grey's case, because he was a candid man with comparatively simple beliefs, the links are fairly obvious, but in other cases they may be harder to trace. Can we, for example, find out something about French political attitudes by studying the exercises in classical rhetoric to which pupils in French *lycées* were subjected? And how far did the Prussian regulations of 1889 which stressed the need for greater attention to recent German history, in order to demonstrate "that the power of the State alone can protect the individual, his family, his freedom and his rights," condition the attitudes of a whole generation? Here is a field in which historians should welcome co-operation with educational sociologists and social psychologists.

A study of educational systems and their content may help to explain the actions and unspoken motives of statesmen and generals in moments of crisis. But what is even harder for the historian is to re-create the whole climate of opinion within which political leaders in the past operated, and to discover what were the assumptions in the minds of ordinary men and women faced with the consequences of their rulers' decisions. In 1914 this is perhaps particularly difficult. People acted on a number of

contradictory assumptions or half-formu-
lated philosophies of life. Some of them,
when war was imminent, felt themselves
caught up in an ineluctable historical process—an age-old conflict between Germans
and Slavs, for instance, which was the view
of the younger Moltke, Chief of the German
General Staff at the outbreak of war. Others
felt themselves to be following a course laid
down by an inexplicable God. "If you see
me so calm," the Tsar said, once the decision
to mobilise the Russian army had been taken,
"it is because I have a firm and resolute faith
that the fate of Russia, of myself and of my
family is in the hands of God who has placed
me where I am. Whatever happens, I shall
bow to His will conscious of having had no
other thought than that of serving the
country He has entrusted to me." Others
simply could not accept the collapse of years
of liberal hopes of international conciliation
and international solidarity. Many people
felt that the fabric of international life had
been too tightly and intricately woven for it
to be broken by war. As the Belgian Socialist
leader Émile Vandervelde said in 1911:
"There are in Europe at present too many
pacifist forces, starting with the Jewish
capitalists who give financial support to
many governments, through to the socialists
who are firmly resolved to prevent mobilisation of the nations and in the event of defeat
to spring at the throats of their rulers." If
the positive force of international co-operation was not enough, then the fear of chaos
and revolution ought to serve to prevent
war. For many people all over Europe, it was
impossible not to be optimistic and not to
hope for the best. As Jean Jaurès remarked a
day or two before he was assassinated by a
nationalist fanatic, *"Les choses ne peuvent
ne pas s'arranger"*—"Things must turn out all
right."

It was Jaurès nevertheless who had seen
most clearly where a European war might
lead. In 1905, when for the first time for
years war between France and Germany
seemed a real possibility, he had written:
"From a European war a revolution may
spring up and the ruling classes would do
well to think of this. But it may also result,

over a long period, in a crisis of counter-
revolution, of furious reaction, of exasper-
ated nationalism, of stifling dictatorship, of
monstrous militarism, a long chain of retro-
grade violence. . . ." Fear of revolution, however, could work both ways; while it might
sometimes prevent governments from risking
a war, more often war seemed a way of
averting revolution by an appeal to deeper
national loyalties. Certainly, both in France
and Germany the fact that, when war came,
the Socialists gave it their positive support
was an important element in the sense of
relief which many people experienced once
war had begun.

In a very few cases—that of Austria-
Hungary is the clearest—the idea of war as a
means of escape from insoluble internal
difficulties played a positive and conscious
part in the decisions of July 1914. But in
nearly all the belligerent countries the outbreak of war meant a temporary cessation of
domestic politics and the establishment of
an *Union Sacrée,* of a *Burgfriede*. Even in
Britain, as the crisis became more serious,
Asquith, the Prime Minister, wrote—correctly—"It is the most dangerous situation of
the last fifty years. It may incidentally have
the effect of throwing into the background
the lurid pictures of civil war in Ulster."

In general, it could perhaps be said that
for every man who foresaw a black future in
July and August 1914, there were, in each
belligerent country, at least as many who
saw in the war a release from public and
private tensions. The enthusiasm which
greeted the war, however, went beyond a
sense of relief at the diversion or postponement of political disputes. Nor was it limited
to militarists like the German Crown Prince
with his notorious summons *"Auf zu einem
frisch-fröhlichen Krieg"*—in itself, incidentally, perhaps no worse than Secretary John
Hay's description of the Spanish-American
War of 1898 as "a splendid little war." The
great historian Friedrich Meinecke declared
that August 1914 was "one of the great
moments of my life which suddenly filled
my soul with the deepest confidence in our
people and the profoundest joy." And in

England there were young writers who felt much the same thing:

> Honour has come back, as a king, to earth
> And paid his subjects with a royal wage;
> And nobleness walks in our ways again;
> And we have come into our heritage.

How can we explain these different reactions to the coming of war? And can we link the attitudes that underlie them to the specific decisions of politicians, diplomats or generals? Or, in other words, what is the connection between the history of ideas and the history of international politics? Is there any point in trying to find one? It is tempting, for instance, to see whether there are links between the art of a society and its political attitudes and to follow the suggestion of Sir Joshua Reynolds, who held that the character of a nation is, perhaps, more strongly marked by their taste in painting than in any other pursuit although more considerable; as you may easier find which way the wind sits by throwing a straw in the air than any heavier substance. One would like to be able to relate, for example, the passionate desperation of Alban Berg's *Three Orchestral Pieces*, Opus 6, on which he was working in August 1914, to the European crisis, or to be able to say that the fragmentation of the image introduced into European painting by Picasso and Braque after 1907 somehow reflects the break-up of bourgeois society. I am sceptical about the possibility of talking in this way with any degree of precision, and, in the case of Berg, his despair seems to have been the result of a quarrel with his master, Schönberg, rather than of public events towards which, indeed, he took a conventional Austrian patriotic attitude. It is interesting to note, however, that so distinguished a historian as Sir Llewellyn Woodward takes the view that there is a direct historical connection between art and society. In the introduction to his recent work on *Great Britain and the War of 1914-1918*, where he writes of his own youth before the First World War, he says: "I neither understood nor sympathised with the new fashion in imaginative writing. I continued to think of the barbarians infiltrating into and finally overthrowing the high civilisation of the western Roman Empire. . . .When I looked at the latest modes in painting I thought of the curious forecast made by the Abbé Lamennais over a century ago about an atheist society falling into ruin in spite of its immense material achievements: 'Reason will decay before men's eyes. The simplest truths will appear strange and remarkable and will scarcely be endured.' " Historians of a younger generation mostly now take for granted and even admit to enjoying the literary and artistic developments which Sir Llewellyn deplores, but there are no doubt some among them—of whom I am definitely not one—who are equally ready to see in the advanced artistic manifestations of the 1960s the same signs of decay as Sir Llewellyn recalls noting half a century ago. One is tempted to say that from Plato onwards it has been conservatives who have been readiest to look to the arts for signs of decadence in society, until one remembers the discussions in socialist and communist circles about social realism, and is forced to conclude that philistinism is not the prerogative of any one political movement.

In an ideal syllabus for a course in International History there would certainly be provision for the study of international artistic movements as well as of the history of international politics, but in our present attempt to discover the unspoken assumptions of the ruling classes and political leaders in Europe in 1914, I do not think that a study of the best art and literature of the time will get us very far; and the historian would certainly be hard put to it to trace any significant links between Berg and Berchtold or between Picasso and President Poincaré. The truth is that if we want to reconstruct the intellectual climate of an age, it is not to the newest or most original writers and artists to whom we must turn. We can see now, for instance, that Freud or Einstein were among the most interesting and important figures of the years immediately before 1914, but it is only after several decades that popularised versions of their ideas have entered into the *Weltanschauung* of the ordinary man and affected the general climate of opinion, just as it has taken many years for the pictorial discoveries of, say, a Klee or a Mondrian to influence the images with which the mass media surround us. Although Arthur Balfour or R. B. Haldane might claim some knowledge of German philosophy, or Clemenceau be on friendly terms with Monet and Debussy, most of the members of the ruling classes of Europe before 1914 were acting on ideas and assumptions formulated twenty or thirty years before, and took little interest in advanced ideas or artistic developments.

If we want to understand the presuppositions of the men of 1914, to reconstruct, so to speak, their ideological furniture, it is to the ideas of a generation earlier, as filtered through vulgarisers and popularisers, that we must look. Let me give one or two examples. It is a commonplace that Darwinian ideas had a great influence on the ideology of Imperialism at the end of the nineteenth century, but it is important to realise how literally the doctrine of the struggle for existence and of the survival of the fittest—a doctrine that owes as much to T. H. Huxley as to Darwin—was taken by many European leaders just before the First World War. Here is a passage, for instance, from the memoirs of the Austrian Chief of the General Staff, Franz Baron Conrad von Hötzendorf: "Philanthropic religions," he wrote, "moral teachings and philosophical doctrines may certainly sometimes serve to weaken mankind's struggle for existence in its crudest form, but they will *never* succeed in removing it as a driving motive in the world. . . .It is in accordance with this great principle that the catastrophe of the World War came about inevitably and irresistibly as the result of the motive forces in the lives of States and peoples, like a thunderstorm which must by its nature discharge itself." Seen against this sort of ideological background, Conrad's continuous insistence on the need for a preventive war in order to preserve the Austro-Hungarian Monarchy is much more comprehensible.

The doctrine of a perpetual struggle for survival and of a permanent potential war of all against all is one with natural attractions for soldiers, who are failing in their duty if they are not actively preparing for just such a clash. But the pseudo-Darwinian view of international society extended to civilians as well. Kurt Riezler, for example, the personal assistant and confidant of the German Chancellor, Bethmann-Hollweg, was a highly sophisticated and intelligent writer about international affairs—and his book on *Principles of World Policy* published under a pseudonym just before the First World War foreshadows some of our own thinking about peace and war today. But underlying Riezler's cool analysis and realistic appraisal of forces and events is a firm conviction that States are living organisms, driven by their inner nature into conflicts with each other, conflicts which may be postponed by diplomacy, or delayed as long as there is enough unallocated living-space in the world to allow for peaceful competition, but which may easily take the form of total war. The view of international society which Riezler implicitly accepts himself, after examining alternative conceptions, is stated by him as follows: "Eternal and absolute enmity is fundamentally inherent in relations between peoples; and the hostility which we observe everywhere and which refuses to disappear from political life, however much the pacifists may speak or struggle against it, is not the result of a perversion of human nature but of the essence of the world and the source of life itself. It is not accidental, temporary and removable, but a necessity which may perhaps be put off for centuries and fall into the background, but which will break out again and claim its place as long as there are men and nations." This kind of thinking in the intimate circle of the German Chancellor perhaps explains Bethmann-Hollweg's fatalistic acceptance of the risk of war inherent in his policy, and of the ultimate inevitability of armed conflict. In this connection it is worth noting, as Dr. Imanuel Geiss has pointed out, that it is possibly from another essay by Riezler that Bethmann-Hollweg took the notorious phrase "a scrap of paper" with which he described the treaty guaranteeing Belgium.

"We make treaties of arbitration," Riezler had written, "and we develop a new international law, but events constantly prove how easily international paper is torn up. . . .In a struggle in which all are involved and consideration for the onlooker abandoned, all conventions will be in vain."

One could produce many more examples of this kind of thinking from other countries as well as from Germany and Austria-Hungary. When Lord Milner died, for example, a *Credo* was found among his papers containing the significant phrase "A Nationalist believes that this is the law of human progress, that the competition between nations each seeking its maximum development, is the Divine Order of the World, the Law of life and progress." I only want to suggest that one cannot understand the outlook on international relations of the generation of 1914 without taking into account the pseudo-Darwinian element in their ideas. Many historians have recognised this, but it would be valuable to have a systematic study of the dissemination and perversion of Darwin's ideas in the fifty-five years between the publication of *The Origin of Species* and the outbreak of the First World War.

The other thinker who is all-important for the understanding of the moral and intellectual climate of 1914 is, of course, Friedrich Nietzsche, and here again it would be valuable to have a study of the translation and dissemination of his works and of the writings about him on the lines of Geneviève Bianquis's book, *Nietzsche en France,* written some forty years ago, and the recent work by Gonzalo Sobejano on *Nietzsche en España.* When Nietzsche finally collapsed into madness in 1889, he was little read; by the time of his death in 1900 he was already a figure of European importance whose teachings were being quoted, misquoted and interpreted in a number of different ways, and in the years before 1914 no one with any intellectual pretensions was ignorant of his work. During the war itself, in 1917, 140,000 copies were sold of the pocket edition of *Also sprach Zarathustra,* and in England at least, as Desmond MacCarthy

pointed out in 1914, he was somehow already vaguely held responsible for the war. Certainly, his ideas, often misunderstood, taken out of context or perverted, contributed to the acceptance of the idea of war not just as a lamentable episode in international relations but as an experience desirable and salutary in itself. "There will be wars as never before on earth," Nietzsche had written. "With me begins on earth High Politics." (*"Erst von mir an gibt es auf Erden Grosse Politik."*) Nietzsche's ideas contributed to the fulfillment of his own prophecies.

But, of course, while some members of the government élite in Germany and some nationalist thinkers in France were affected by Nietzsche's teaching in one form or another, these ideas were even more important to those who were preparing to overthrow the existing social order. The impact of ideas is always greater on revolutionaries than on supporters of the established system, and, before 1914, in some parts of Europe at least, students, as now, were eager for fresh ideas which would justify their restless desire for action and for new forms of thought and expression. If politicians and bureaucrats are influenced by the doctrines of a generation earlier, student rebels seize eagerly on any ideas which are in the air and which seem to be the most advanced, and Nietzsche, although much of his writing had appeared some thirty years before, was still thought of as the inspirer of the *avant-garde*. The fascinating investigation which Dr. Vladimir Dedijer has conducted into the background, beliefs and origins of the Young Bosnia movement, from which the assassins of the Archduke Franz Ferdinand came, has shown how, for these Serb students, half-understood philosophical principles were quickly transformed into action, and how advanced ideas about politics and art, litera[t]ure and life were inextricably confused and contributed to a passionate sense of excitement and commitment. As one of the intellectual inspirers of the southern Slav radicals wrote: "Thought, free thought, is the greatest and bravest ruler of the universe. It has huge space wings of the freest and most audacious bird, for which fear and danger do not exist. Its wild flight goes to infinity and eternity. It destroys today what was created yesterday. It destroys every dogma, every norm, every authority. It has no other faith but the faith in its power. It creates critics, subversives, rebels and wreckers." These ideas, with their echoes of the Nietzschean "reversal of all values," were what inspired the young men who murdered the Archduke and his wife and precipitated the crisis of 1914; and it is no surprise to learn that Princip, the actual assassin, was fond of reciting Nietzsche's short poem *Ecce Homo,* with its lines "Insatiable as flame, I burn and consume myself."

Again, the café intellectuals who supported Mussolini, himself an eager reader of Nietzsche, when, in the early months of the war, he left the Italian Socialist Party to become one of the main agitators in favour of intervention, and who took as one of their slogans *"Guerra, sola igiene del mondo"* (War, the only hygiene for the world), were voicing ideas which they thought they had found in Nietzsche. Even the poet Rainer Maria Rilke—not usually a writer to whom one turns for echoes of contemporary political or public events—combines Nietzschean language, to which he was always responsive, with a sense of the prevailing excitement on the outbreak of war, in his *Fünf Gesänge:*

Andere sind wir, ins Gleiche geänderte: jedem sprang in die plötzlich
nicht mehr seinige Brust meteorisch ein Herz.
Heiss ein eisernes Herz aus eisernem Weltall.

("We are different beings transformed into the same: suddenly like a meteor a heart leapt into the breast no more one's own. Hot, an iron heart in an iron universe.")

Ideas and images of this kind contributed, it seems to me, to a climate in which the fact of war was not just regretfully accepted but, by many people, positively welcomed. Walther Rathenau was not the only one to find August 1914, in his own words: "Great and unforgettable. It was the ringing opening chord for an immortal song

of sacrifice, loyalty and heroism." And even a man who was already pessimistic about the situation, such as General von Falkenhayn, the Prussian War Minister who was soon to become Chief of the General Staff, was sufficiently impressed by the grandeur of events to exclaim on 4 August, "Even if we end in ruin, it was beautiful."

The sense of inevitability and the sense of relief, as the crisis mounted and as war came, were partly due, as I suggested earlier, to the technical sequence of mobilisation plans and to the fact that politicians, even if they wanted to, could not stop the military machine once it was in motion, and partly to the fact that many of Europe's leaders saw in the international crisis a distraction from internal problems. But it is also due, I suggest, to the fact that by 1914 the ideas both of Darwin and of Nietzsche had become widely assimilated, so that there were many people in Europe, both among rulers and ruled, who thought of life in terms of the struggle for survival, or who were looking for an opportunity to transcend the limitations of their ordinary lives and to find a new set of values in what they believed would be a new and enriching experience.

Lloyd George made the somewhat pedestrian point in his *War Memoirs* that "War has always been fatal to liberalism. Peace, Retrenchment and Reform have no meaning in war." If one stands back from the details of the crisis of 1914 and thinks about some of the ideas prevalent in Europe at the time, the outbreak of the First World War can be seen as a defeat for those in all the belligerent countries who believed in the application of reason to the settlement of disputes, who believed that all problems have solutions, and that international goodwill and co-operation would suffice to prevent war. This is the attitude, for all their differences, both of the socialist leaders assembled in Brussels on 29 and 30 July 1914, planning to organise an international congress for the following week to discuss the measures to be taken against war, and of Sir Edward Grey, interrupting his Sunday's fishing to authorise, from his cottage at Itchen Abbas, the dispatch of a telegram suggesting a Conference of Ambassadors in London "in order to find an issue to present complications."

If we are to understand the conflicting beliefs which lie behind the actions of statesmen and the reactions of their followers, we must look at a number of ideas, attitudes and assumptions which are not always to be found in the archives. And one could of course suggest many other lines of approach in addition to the rather obvious ones I have proposed. These might be philosophical: how much, if anything, for example, did the doctrine of the offensive adopted by French military leaders before 1914 owe to a misunderstanding of Bergson's ideas about *élan vital*? Or they might be historical: in what way does the concept of a vital national interest arise or an idea such as that of the "balance of power" develop? "Great revolutions," Hegel wrote, "which strike the eye at a glance must have been preceded by a still and silent revolution in the spirit of the age, a revolution not visible to every eye, especially imperceptible to contemporaries and hard to discern or to describe in words. It is lack of acquaintance with this spiritual revolution which makes the resulting changes astonishing." It is as important for the historian of international relations to understand these changes in what Hegel calls the spirit of the age as it is for him to understand changes in the structure of the economy or developments in military technology.

Sir Charles Webster called his Inaugural Lecture in the Stevenson Chair "The Study of International History," and Professor Medlicott's was entitled "The Scope and Study of International History." I am afraid that by giving this lecture a more specific title I may have implied that I was going to talk about something different, instead of trying to suggest ways of extending the scope and deepening the study of International History. But the crisis of 1914 owes its continuing interest to the fact that it provides an opportunity of trying many different approaches and offering many different types of historical explanation. It is an example of the extent to which what we call International History must in fact embrace all kinds of history, and it suggests that any attempt to insist on a too rigid departmental division of historical studies into economic history, diplomatic history, military history, art history, and so on, must lead to an impoverishment of our historical understanding. Specialists in each branch as well as specialists in other disciplines must help each other if we are to succeed in reconstructing the thought and action of the past. "Since wars begin in the minds of men," the Charter of UNESCO lays down, "it is in the minds of men that the defences of peace must be constructed." This is certainly an aim which Sir Daniel Stevenson would have appreciated. The study of the minds of the men of 1914—whether they deliberately made the war or, as Lloyd George claimed to believe, stumbled into it—is of obvious intrinsic historical interest, but I also believe that by studying the origins of a particular war we may contribute to the understanding of situations likely to cause other wars and to the understanding of the causes of war in general. But, in any case, it is only by studying the minds of men that we shall understand the causes of anything.

Zara Steiner

THE VIEW FROM LONDON:
BRITAIN'S DECISION TO FIGHT

Germany, Austria-Hungary, and possibly Russia: these three powers most often stand accused of having been responsible for the war of 1914. Yet from the start of that conflict German writers, but others elsewhere as well, argued that had Britain clarified its intention to intervene, Berlin would never have plunged forward. Further, it is the question of Britain and what Britain would do that forms a major theme through all Fischer's writings.

British policy was probably neither so benign as Fischer would aver nor so deliberately Machiavellian as earlier critics, including Harry Elmer Barnes, alleged. Rather it was more complex and contradictory, at once cautious and defensive, at once assertive and self-righteous, at once straightforward and yet with a touch of mendacity, especially in publicly defining its relationship with France.

No work better synthesizes both recent historical study on British involvement and the larger historical debate than Zara Steiner's *Britain and the Origins of the First World War*. An American trained at Radcliffe and Harvard and now a fellow at New Hall, Cambridge University, Dr. Steiner established her reputation in the late 1960s as a student of the British Foreign Office. In her newest book she incorporates the diplomatic world into the larger political and social framework. The result is an analysis which shows Great Britain in a more participatory, less passive role than most of the historiography since Fritz Fischer would suggest. In short, London was an actor in the drama of 1914.

VIEWED from London, the July crisis falls into two unequal parts. Throughout the weeks of July, Grey concentrated on bringing about a diplomatic solution of the Serbian crisis. For the most part, he worked alone without heeding the advice of his permanent officials or giving undue consideration to the varying opinions held by the Cabinet or party. When it appeared to the Foreign Secretary that war was inevitable, the battle for intervention shifted to the Cabinet. Grey had always believed that the country would have to defend France in a Franco-German conflict; he now had to convince those who had never really accepted this conclusion. It is only by considering both stages in Grey's diplomacy that one can understand why Britain, though legally and technically free, dispatched an ultimatum to the Germans. One must answer the even more troubling question as to why, given the divided state of the Liberals, to say nothing of the country at large, people went willingly to war and maintained their en-

From Zara Steiner, *Britain and the Origins of the First World War* (New York: St. Martin's Press, 1977), pp. 220-239. Used by permission of St. Martin's Press.

thusiasm after the terrible battles of 1914 and 1915.

Almost from the start, Grey realised the gravity of the new crisis. The death of the Archduke roused considerable sympathy for the Dual Monarchy and when the editors and leader-writers returned from their interrupted weekend, almost all laid the blame for the deed on those "impossible Serbians." At the Foreign Office, it was assumed that the Serbians were involved but that not much would come of the affair. But Lichnowsky, who had returned home for a short visit during Kiel week, saw Grey on 6 July and warned him that the Austrians intended to take strong measures and the Germans would support them. He seems to have spoken quite freely with the Foreign Secretary. He had been worried by the mood of "anxiety and pessimism" he had found in Berlin. The fear of Russian armaments and the news of the Anglo-Russian naval talks had created a feeling that "trouble was bound to come and therefore it would be better not to restrain Austria and let trouble come now rather than later." There is every indication that Grey took the ambassador's warnings seriously. The latter's information confirmed Grey's own reading of the divisions in the Kaiser's entourage. Lichnowsky had been instructed to underline the dangers of victory for the militarists; Albert Ballin, who arrived in London in the middle of the crisis, repeated the same message to Grey and Haldane at a dinner party on 23 July.

Grey's strategy was clear. In the event of a fresh crisis in the Balkans the British would work with the German government "as far as might be possible" without moving away from France and Russia. This was the policy Grey followed throughout the early weeks of the Sarajevo drama. On the 9th the German ambassador was told, "I would continue the same policy as I had pursued through the Balkan crisis. . . .The greater the risk of war the more closely would I adhere to this policy." Grey was, perhaps, "a little over-flattered by the success of the Balkan Conference the year before" but he genuinely felt that the Germans would restrain their allies if reassured about Russian intentions. For his part, Grey asked the French and the Russians to do everything possible to defuse the situation. Without revealing the source of his anxiety, so as to avoid demands for diplomatic support, he warned that an aroused public in Vienna would demand satisfaction. The strength of this warning was weakened when Nicolson, who had still not taken the measure of the crisis, assured Cambon that Grey was over-anxious and paying too much attention to German complaints about Anglo-Russian relations.

Meanwhile, the Austrians sought German backing on 5 July; the Kaiser's blank cheque was backed by demands for a rapid settlement of the Serbian affair. The Kaiser left for Kiel on the morning of the sixth and on the following day departed for Norwegian waters abroad the *Hohenzollern.* Moltke continued his cure at Carlsbad and Tirpitz his holiday in the Black Forest. Rumours of impending action were reaching London. De Bunsen, reporting from Vienna, found that "a kind of indictment" was being prepared against Serbia with the full support of Germany. As it became clear that Germany might not play the same role as in 1912, Grey began to take alarm. He advised the Russian and Austrian governments to discuss the Serbian problem between themselves, a proposal which reached St. Petersburg during Poincaré's state visit. The President and Sazanov preferred a warning of the Entente powers at Vienna but Grey was reluctant to make a demonstration of Entente solidarity which would alarm the Germans and involve Britain in an Austro-Serbian quarrel. Even the Foreign Office, now apprised of the seriousness of the situation, cautioned against joint intervention in Vienna.

On 24 July the Foreign Office was given the text of the ultimatum delivered at Belgrade the day before. Grey found it "the most formidable document I have ever seen addressed by one State to another that was independent." The Foreign Office was now up in arms. Crowe insisted that the Austrian action changed the entire complexion of the case which no longer was a question of the Austrian charges against Serbia. "The moment has passed when it might have been possible to enlist French support in an effort to hold back Russia. . . .France and Russia consider that these are the pretexts and that the bigger cause of Triple Alliance versus Triple Entente is definitely engaged. . . .Our interests are tied up with those of France and Russia in this struggle, which is not for the possession of Serbia, but one between Germany aiming at political dictatorship in Europe and the Powers who desire, to retain individual freedom." But if Crowe spoke for a Foreign Office group, Grey ignored his advice. He continued to hope that Beth-mann-Hollweg and Jagow would restrain their chauvinists and bring the Austrians to the bargaining table.

At the close of the [Cabinet] discussions on Ulster on the afternoon of 24 July, Grey brought up the Serbian crisis. Until this time the Foreign Secretary had consulted only Asquith, Haldane and Churchill; he had no wish to involve the pacifist wing of the Cabinet. "The parishes of Fermanagh and Tyrone faded back into the mists and squalls of Ireland and a strange light began immediately but by perceptible gradations to fall and glow upon the map of Europe." This was the first time for a month that the Cabinet discussed foreign policy. Grey suggested that the four less interested powers intervene in case of dangerous tension between Russia and Austria. The Cabinet then scattered for the weekend. Grey went to his fishing-lodge after receiving Cambon and Lichnowsky to whom he recommended a joint proposal at Vienna to extend the time limit of the ultimatum and the four-power intervention approved by the Cabinet. There was a sense of crisis but it was thought that the situation would be resolved peacefully. Asquith, in particular, was still focused on Ireland; that country was on the verge of a civil war for which the government was ill prepared.

The situation long predicted by Nicolson and Crowe had become a hideous reality. Both men were highly suspicious of the German role. Bethmann had not passed on Grey's suggestion for a four-power intervention. On the Sunday of this first crisis weekend (26 July) Nicolson, left in the Office while Grey went fishing, proposed a four-power conference in London. With the Foreign Secretary's approval, telegrams were dispatched to the respective European capitals. Nicolson, personally, would have preferred an open declaration of support for the Entente. He feared the consequences of Grey's holding policy particularly when the Serbian answer was rejected and the Austrians began military preparations. He and Crowe brought increasing pressure on the Foreign Secretary to take a more determined stand. Grey refused to be rushed. When he returned to London on Sunday evening, Churchill told him that the fleet had been kept together after the Spithead Review. The Foreign Secretary agreed that publicising the decision might soothe the Russians and the French and serve as a useful warning to Germany and Austria. But he had not given up hopes for a settlement through Berlin.

The uncertain public mood undoubtedly had some bearing on his outlook. The Conservative press, at the start, had joined the anti-Serbian chorus. Even after the ultimatum, there were papers on both sides of the political fence which found the Austrian measures justified. After the publication of the Serbian reply, the press mood began to stiffen and split along party lines. *The Times,* despite a German-Austrian campaign to influence its editors, took the lead in demanding a strong stand and participation in the coming war. Gradually, the whole Tory press followed suit. The Liberal journals, on the other hand, particularly the *Manchester Guardian,* possibly briefed by Lloyd George, *Daily News* and *Standard,* denounced the campaign of the "Thunderer" and recommended a policy of strict neutrality. "We care as little for Belgrade," a typical leader read, "as Belgrade for Manchester." Those who opposed participation did so for the most diverse reasons. There were pacifists and radicals, anti-Russians and pro-Germans, City men and manufacturers. Though undoubtedly aware of these varying views and the strength of the anti-war forces, Grey's thinking was only marginally affected. Tyrrell, his loyal secretary, had a sharp passage of arms with Valentine Chirol over the attitude of *The Times* but Grey maintained his public detachment.

Despite this appearance of calm, the Foreign Secretary realised that he could no longer ignore his political colleagues. At a full meeting of the Cabinet on the 27th, Grey raised the issue of participation in a form which he thought would bring him the widest range of support. Would the government enter a war if France were attacked by Germany? Burns, Morley, Simon, Beauchamp and Harcourt warned that they would resign if such a decision was taken. It was agreed to dispatch warning telegrams to all naval, military and colonial stations initiating a "precautionary period." The Admiralty's decision to postpone the dispersal of the First and Second fleets was approved. The question of Belgian neutrality would be considered at the next cabinet meeting. Nothing further could be done. The equivocal position of his colleagues encouraged Grey to again press Germany to restrain her ally. The Foreign Secretary continued to hope that under the influence of the German Chancellor the government would use its power to preserve the peace. But he had strong doubts and needed to prepare the Cabinet for an adverse conclusion to his efforts. On the 27th, in a conversation with Lichnowsky, Grey voiced his suspicions that Germany was not really interested in mediation and that while he had been urging the Russians along a conciliatory path nothing comparable was being done in Vienna.

Grey's fears were all too well founded. Bethmann had forwarded, without comment, Grey's request that Germany advise Austria not to make war on Serbia. On 27 July, the Germans rejected the four-power conference proposal though they recorded their support for mediation in principle. Grey held his hand hoping that the newly started Austro-Russian conversations in St. Petersburg might produce favourable results. On the 28th, after the Austrian declaration of war on Serbia, the talks ceased. The Germans had waited anxiously until the Austrians had delivered their ultimatum at Belgrade. The bombardment of the Serbian

capital was greeted with relief. Bethmann was now mainly concerned with the two-week gap which would follow before the Austrian army was ready to proceed. Grey's policy of non-alignment had little influence on these developments. British mediation between the two power groups had not prevented an Austrian war against Serbia. It was not British but Austrian and German policy which distinguished this crisis from that of 1912. The working partnership of the Balkan Wars was not revived because the Central Powers had other goals in mind.

Civil war in Ireland drew closer as the Irish Volunteers successfully mounted their first gun-running expedition at Howth on Sunday 26 July. Soldiers attempting to disarm the Volunteers opened fire on a Dublin crowd attacking them with bottles and stones. Three civilians were killed and thirty-eight injured at Bachelor's Walk. Nevertheless, cabinet attention was riveted on Europe. On the 29th, after a long evening meeting with Asquith and Haldane, Grey conferred with his other colleagues. John Burns summed up the sitiation: "critical cabinet at 11:30. . . . Situation seriously reviewed from all points of view. It was decided not to decide." Grey, drained of optimism, advocated a promise of support for France. He was seconded by Asquith, Churchill, Haldane and Crewe but opposed by all the rest. Both the French and the Germans were to be told, "we were unable to pledge ourselves in advance, either under all condition to stand aside or in any condition to go in." On the question of Belgian neutrality, the Cabinet, like Gladstone's in 1870, decided that the obligation to uphold the 1839 Treaty fell on all the signatory powers collectively but not on any single one individually. If the matter arose, the decision would be "one of policy rather than legal obligation." Despite the Cabinet's caution, Grey gave Lichnowsky a private warning that if Germany and France went to war, Britain could not "stand aside and wait for any length of time." Yet he told Cambon that the country was "free from engagements, and we should have to decide what British interests required us to do." Cambon was indignant, Nicolson and Crowe in a state of panic. The next day, the 30th, Bonar Law and Carson, on their own initiative, saw Asquith who agreed to postpone the second reading of the Home Rule Amending Bill. It was the one "bright spot" in a dreadful day.

In every European capital, military considerations began to influence diplomatic calculations. In St. Petersburg the government decided to mobilise the military districts of Kiev, Odessa, Moscow and Kazan. The military chiefs and Sazonov, feeling that a partial mobilisation left Russia unprotected against Germany, were already urging the Tsar to agree to total mobilisation. There followed a period of hesitation and even a withdrawal of the mobilisation order until the Tsar made his final decision on the 30th. It seems a doubtful proposition to assign undue importance to this final act though it enabled the German government to proclaim publicly that it was fighting a defensive war. What was important was the Russian determination not to accept a Serbian defeat at Austrian hands. Both Berchtold and Bethmann realised that Austrian military action was almost bound to provoke a Russian military response which would result in the calling up of all the armies of Europe. Unless the Central Powers would accept a diplomatic compromise, which their leaders considered a defeat, Russian mobilisation meant that the war could not be localised. The Serbians, too, counted on a positive Russian reaction. Not even the Kaiser's intervention after his return to Berlin on the 27th could reverse the situation; Bethmann had gone too far to desert the Austrians whom he had been urging to act. Moltke prepared for war; Bethmann, in a mood of "hopeless despondency" according to his secretary, recovered sufficiently to mobilise the nation for the impending clash. There remained the question of Britain.

It has been argued that a blunt statement to Germany on 26 July that Britain would intervene on the side of France would have deterred the Chancellor from pushing Austria into her Serbian war. There has been considerable debate among German historians whether Bethmann counted on British

neutrality. Bethmann and Jagow may have hoped that Grey would delay long enough to allow the German army time to make its intended break through Belgium. On 29 July, while Grey was having his critical conversation with Lichnowsky which was to crush whatever illusions Bethmann still harboured, there was a Crown Council at Potsdam. Prince Henry reported that the King of England had given his word that "England will remain neutral in the event of war." The German Emperor chose to discount the news that Grey had warned the Prince: "the matter would be different if we were to crush France." On his return from Potsdam, Bethmann summoned Goschen and made his bid for British neutrality. The German Chancellor promised that if Germany defeated France, French territorial integrity would be maintained but refused to extend his pledge to cover the French colonies. He could offer no guarantee of Belgian neutrality. "The only comment that need be made on these astounding proposals," Crowe minuted, "is that they reflect discredit on the statesmen who make them. . . .It is clear that Germany is practically determined to go to war, and that the one restraining influence so far has been the fear of England joining in the defence of France and Belgium." Grey agreed that the Chancellor's proposals could "not for a moment be entertained." Despite his fury, he made one last effort to reassure Berlin to get the powers to the conference table. By the 30th, Bethmann was interested only in Britain's neutrality. Yet he had been temporarily shaken by Lichnowsky's report of Grey's warning on the 29th, a warning which the Cabinet had not authorised and could have been given at any stage in the crisis. This report reached Berlin in the late hours of the 30th, crossing with Bethmann's clumsy neutrality offer. What followed was shadow-boxing rather than diplomacy.

Vienna was advised to "stop in Belgrade" and Grey was told that every effort would be made to get the Austrians to accept his mediation proposals. Grey backed a parallel stand at St. Petersburg on the 30th and 31st. The Foreign Secretary seems not to have understood the full significance of Russian mobilisation and did not anticipate the immediate German reaction on the 31st. That evening, the German Emperor offered to restrain Austria if Britain persuaded Russia to delay full mobilisation. Grey, Churchill and Asquith woke the King at one-thirty on 1 August to appeal directly to the Tsar. This move, like all the others, came too late. With mobilisation in Europe, and Germany's ultimatum to Russia on 31 July, war had become a reality.

The speed of the crisis and the rapid resort to arms threw the British off balance. But Grey had followed the wrong course during July. He had hoped until the very end that by not coming down on either side, he would delay the adoption of extreme measures. He felt personally deceived, "outraged at the way Germany and Austria have played with the most vital interests of civilization, have put aside all attempts at accommodation made by himself and others, and while continuing to negotiate have marched steadily to war." Grey was convinced, both at the time and in later years, that the blame lay with the German militarists. "Jagow did nothing, Bethmann-Hollweg trifled and the military intended war and forced it," the shattered Foreign Secretary wrote in March 1915. This separation between "good" and "bad" Germans, already a part of British official thinking, became an orthodoxy which influenced post-war diplomacy.

We have already suggested that the German actions were only indirectly influenced by British behaviour. Even if Grey had firmly aligned himself with the Dual Alliance, it is not at all clear that this would have had a deterring effect on Berlin. Grey exaggerated his ability to play a "floating role." Though he never intended to abandon his friends, by attempting to mediate between the groups of powers, he may have encouraged Bethmann to gamble on his ultimate neutrality. Grey's semi-detached position left doors open; hence the importance of making Russia appear as the aggressor. Yet Grey was committed to upholding the equilibrium in Europe which meant supporting the French and the Russians. The Foreign Secretary was both the beneficiary and the prisoner of his own system. It was for this reason that though the war was a personal defeat from which Grey did not recover, he never believed that there was an alternative policy.

One is struck by the singular independence of the Foreign Secretary. The Foreign Office as a department was totally impotent. All who could stayed in London that final fateful weekend wanting to help but did not know how. Contemporary accounts record the sense of frustration and despair with which the senior officials watched the course of events. From the time the terms of the Austrian ultimatum had become known, Nicolson and Crowe believed war was inevitable. Nicolson was concerned with the preservation of the Russian Entente; Crowe with the German threat. Neither man could persuade Grey to abandon his efforts in Berlin. It was less a question of officials being anti-Austrian than of assuming that Austria was Germany's pawn in a much larger game. Nicolson wanted a statement of support for Russia; Crowe a declaration of solidarity with the Entente powers. The latter hoped that a show of naval force as soon as any power mobilised might avoid a conflagration. Yet even during the critical weekend of 25-26 July, Grey was unwilling to adopt his officials' policy of a firm commitment.

Crowe feared that the Foreign Secretary was not qualified by upbringing or study to understand what was going on in the sinister depths of the German mind. The Foreign Office thought the Cabinet would refuse to act. On the 31st, Crowe prepared a respectful but concise review of the British position aimed at strengthening Grey's stand. "The argument that there is no written bond binding us to France is strictly correct. There is no contractual obligation. But the Entente has been made, strengthened, put to the test and celebrated in a manner justifying the beliefs that a moral bond was being forged. . .Our duty and our interest will be seen to lie in standing by France. . . ." Crowe argued that to remain neutral would imply an abandonment of all past policies.

"The theory that England cannot engage in a big war means her abdication as an independent state. . . .A balance of power cannot be maintained by a State that is incapable of fighting and consequently carries no weight." By the time Crowe wrote this memorandum, Grey was in agreement with his Under-Secretary. But by this date, the Cabinet was involved and, with this shift of venue, Crowe's advice was of little value. The Assistant Under-Secretary was in a distraught state. Beneath the civil servant's garb was an intensely engaged individual absolutely certain of where Britain's duty lay.

Nicolson, too, failed to influence Grey's diplomacy. Despite repeated interventions and a series of minutes which could only have irritated Grey, the Permanent Under-Secretary was helpless. Almost in desperation, Nicolson seized on the Belgians as the *casus belli.* After all, the treaty with Belgium created an obligation which every British government was bound to honour. "You will no doubt have read the White Paper," Nicolson later wrote to Hardinge, "but I may tell you quite privately that I passed an anxious 48 hours at one moment. The Cabinet were not prepared to stand by France. . .I was appalled by the outlook—this was on 31 July—and I wrote to Grey in as strong language as possible in regard to our deserting our friends. The Cabinet were at sixes and sevens over the matter, but the majority were in favour of standing aside and with the exception of Winston, the minority were weak." The emergence of the Belgium question had, in Nicolson's view, become essential for the conversion of this majority.

The feeling in the Foreign Office rose as its ability to influence the course of events diminished. The visits of Henry Wilson, who was meeting Conservative leaders in an effort to force the government's hand, heightened tha anguish of his friends. Only William Tyrrell and Arthur Murray, Grey's parliamentary private secretary, seem to have remained close to their chief. The former was sent repeatedly to the German embassy; the latter dined and played billiards with the Foreign Secretary to pass the evening hours. There was no one else at the Foreign Office close enough to assist Grey during these days. The Foreign Secretary did not at first consult his chief advisers; later he was unwilling and then unable to accept their advice. There existed that almost unbridgeable gap between politician and civil servant which ultimately was far more important than the differences between the men involved. Grey remained detached and self-enclosed even when close to the breaking point. There was no confidential private secretary to record Grey's inner thoughts but the sense of singular responsibility pervades his autobiography written eleven years later.

If Grey's officials did not influence him, it could hardly be expected that the military authorities would have had more success. The Foreign Secretary was in constant touch with Churchill, one of the earliest to be warned of the seriousness of the Serbian affair. But Grey remained, as he had always been, curiously obtuse about the military and naval ties between Britain and France. The military chiefs were anxious to prepare for the dispatch of the B.E.F. Yet no C.I.D. meeting was held and no military opinion solicited by this "cursed cabinet." Wilson alerted the Opposition to the possibility that the Asquith government intended to desert the French. He rushed to the Foreign Office and to the French embassy. It was not the first time he had used highly questionable methods to achieve his ends but in this case he proved unsuccessful. The top army echelon believed they were ready for a European war. "What a real piece of luck this war has been as regards Ireland—just averted a Civil War and when it is over we may all be tired of fighting," Sir William Birdwood remarked a few months after war broke out. On 1 August, after a morning cabinet meeting, Grey told a horrified Cambon that the Cabinet refused to propose to Parliament that a B.E.F. should be sent to France if Britain entered the war. Asquith, who held the seals of Secretary of State for War, had already warned the C.I.G.S. that no such force had been promised and Grey made a similar statement to Nicolson. Though Wilson fumed and plotted and the General Staff waited expectantly, they had no real share in the decision-making process.

The navy was more fortunate in its civilian leadership. Churchill acted on his own initiative. On 29 July, the Cabinet agreed to the First Lord's request for a precautionary mobilisation of the fleet. On the same evening, Churchill interpreted Asquith's "hard stare" and "sort of grunt" as permission to send the fleet to war stations. On 1 August, the First Lord, despite the opposition of the Cabinet though with Asquith's tacit approval, mobilised his navy. It was a symbol of Grey's innocence or stupidity in such matters that it was Cambon who raised the question of Britain's naval commitments to France at that difficult Saturday meeting of the 1st. Cambon insisted that France had pulled back her troops from the frontier to satisfy British public opinion. She had concentrated her fleet in the Mediterranean and left her northern and western coasts exposed. Grey denied the ambassador's contention that the naval arrangements created an obligation to fight particularly as France was going to war because of its Russian alliance, the terms of which Grey did not even know. Nevertheless, Grey promised to bring the naval question before the Cabinet on the 2nd.

This meeting turned out to be the crucial one. It was only then that some ministers seem to have realised that there was some kind of duty to protect the Channel coast of France and that the safety of Britain would be threatened by a Franco-German naval conflict in the Channel. For reasons which will be further explored, it was agreed on that hot, muggy Sunday to promise the French and warn the Germans that the British would not tolerate German naval action in the Channel or against the French coasts. The idea of a naval war was more acceptable than an expeditionary force. This was the one time when the conversations with France affected the Cabinet's decision-making and then it was only of indirect importance as the Germans subsequently promised to refrain from such operations. The political parties had far more influence on the policy-making process than the professionals. Grey knew that he had the support of the Conservative leadership and much of their party. Churchill was already in touch with Bonar Law and F. E. Smith; Henry Wilson had been seeing his friends as well. But, despite these efforts, there was no real move towards coalition. Bonar Law, still concerned with the Government of Ireland Bill, wished to retain his independence. Though the Conservative leader made it clear to Grey that he expected the government to honour its obligations to France, he did warn him "that it was not easy to be sure what the opinion of his whole party was. He doubted whether it would be unanimous or overwhelmingly in favour of war unless Belgian neutrality were involved. In that event he said it would be unanimous." It was due to pressure from Wilson and men like Amery and Milner that the Conservative chiefs offered their unconditional support in a letter which Asquith read to the Cabinet on the morning of the 2nd. There was now the concrete possibility that if the Cabinet split there would be a Coalition or Unionist party leading the country into war.

For Grey, the backing of the Liberal party was essential. The revolt of 1911-1912 had shown that there was considerable feeling against being involved in a European quarrel. Anti-Russian feeling was particularly strong. After its initial pro-Austrian reaction, the Liberal press divided. C. P. Scott began to canvass the radical ministers but in the Commons the radical forces were strangely silent. Parliament was in session but its members were given only scattered bits of information about the escalating crisis. Totally immersed in Irish affairs, the left was caught off balance and could not make the rapid transition to the map of Europe. Most assumed that the government would avoid involvement and stay clear of any Austro-Russian dispute. It was not until the House was about to adjourn for the weekend on 30 July that its members were told that German mobilisation was a distinct possibility. As neither Grey's nor Asquith's abbreviated comments provided much enlightenment, members left in a confused state, their mood somewhat uncertain. C. P. Scott and Arthur Ponsonby took the initiative in mobilising the anti-war forces.

Ponsonby convened meetings of his Foreign Affairs group on each of the last three days of July. On the 29th, he and some ten others prepared a resolution and letter for Grey, warning, "We could not support the Government in any military or naval operation which would carry this country beyond its existing treaty obligation." Grey replied personally to Ponsonby. Though he would make no statement, he assured the chairman that "We are absolutely free and working for peace." The Foreign Secretary asked Ponsonby to keep his group quiet for the week and was himself rather short with those Liberal members who attempted to question him in the House. On the 30th, Ponsonby was instructed to write a sharp letter to Asquith; decision for war "would meet not only with the strongest disapproval but with the actual withdrawal of support from the Government." Ponsonby claimed he represented nine-tenths of the party yet was forced to admit he spoke for some thirty members. Only twenty-two actually attended his meeting. Even those who came were uncertain over the issue of Belgium; it was only as long as no treaty obligations were involved that their veto on participation stood.

As one could have predicted, Asquith made no effort to influence the Ponsonby group and, in fact, was almost totally passive despite his support for Grey. The Foreign Affairs Committee met twice on Friday 31 July, and decided to do nothing until after the weekend. There was endless confusion. Most members continued to trust in Grey's pacific intentions and felt they lacked the necessary information to make an effective protest. By the time Graham Wallas formed his British Neutrality Committee and Norman Angell his Neutrality League on the 28th, it was too late. The feverish radical activity during the weekend was an exercise in futility. The two groups did not merge; declarations to the press and advertisements

in the newspapers came too late to influence cabinet decisions. The first official meeting of the British Neutrality Committee took place on 4 August, its last on the 5th. Less than £20 had been spent. The Neutrality League was more active, but its press announcements appeared between the 3rd and the 5th when the real decisions had been taken.

The Labour party proved to be equally divided and ineffective. The International Socialist Bureau met at Brussels on 29 July but refused to believe that a European war was imminent. On 30 July the parliamentary Labour party unanimously declared that Britain should remain out of the war. The following day, the British section of the International issued a manifesto against war signed by its chairman, Keir Hardie, and its secretary, Arthur Henderson. On Sunday, there were mass meetings and the *International* was sung. Called to Downing Street on Sunday evening, Ramsay MacDonald brought sad tidings to his waiting friends. Yet he told Morley, whom he met in the street, that though he would have nothing to do with war, it "would be the most popular war the country had ever fought." Britain was the only country where the Bank Holiday crowds cheered before the declaration of war.

Was this a revolutionary change of attitude? The Prime Minister wrote to Miss Stanley on 2 August: "I suppose a good 3/4 of our own party in the House of Commons are for absolute non-interference at any price." Even the Conservatives had protesters: Lord Hugh Cecil, for one, "and many silent Tories doubtless feel as impotent and bewildered as the radicals." Most of the population had barely heard of Serbia and certainly did not know where it was. Yet by the 3rd, ministers sensed that the war would be popular. The radicals, divided and kept in ignorance, never effectively focused the anti-war sentiment which existed. Their own equivocation over Belgium provides part of our answer. If the Schlieffen plan had not been implemented, and the Germans had marched eastwards, the situation might have been transformed. But the critical action took place in the Cabinet, not in Parliament, and certainly not in the streets.

Grey repeatedly referred to the essential role of public opinion in his discussions with both the French and the German ambassadors. On 25 July he wrote to Buchanan at St. Petersburg: "I do not consider public opinion here would or ought to sanction our going to war in the Serbian quarrel." Whatever his private feelings about supporting France, Grey in his "rather painful" interview with Cambon on 30 July told the ambassador that public opinion would not support intervention. On the 31st Grey wrote to Goschen: "All I could say was that our attitude would be determined largely by public opinion here, and that the neutrality of Belgium would appeal very strongly to public opinion." Despite these allusions, it was not with the public at large that Grey was concerned but with the Cabinet. The public mood did change. Belgium proved to be a catalyst which unleashed the many emotions, rationalisations and glorifications of war which had long been part of the British climate of opinion. Having a moral cause, all the latent anti-German feeling, fed by years of naval rivalry and assumed enmity, rose to the surface. The "scrap of paper" proved decisive both in maintaining the unity of the government and then in providing a focal point for public feeling. There were important counter-currents yet these were not brought to bear on the one institution which could still reverse Grey's diplomacy and override his decisions. The whole history of the radical movement showed that it was powerless unless it could command a cabinet majority.

The Cabinet had supported Grey's diplomacy all through the Sarajevo crisis. It was only when it came to a decision whether Britain was to enter the war that its divisions became apparent and a battle had to be fought. "The Cabinet was overwhelmingly pacific," Winston Churchill wrote in *The World Crisis.* "At least three-quarters of its members were determined not to be drawn into a European quarrel, unless Great Britain was herself attacked, which was unlikely." Ministerial diaries and letters confirm Churchill's later judgment. On 31 July, Lewis Harcourt passed a note to his colleague, J. A. Pease, "It is now clear that *this* Cabinet will not join in the war." In a second meeting on the same day, the neutralists won a further victory. Churchill's proposal that the fleet reserves be called out and that final preparations for war be made was rejected. Morley and Simon demanded a declaration that in no circumstances would Great Britain be involved in war. Their anti-war views were shared, they claimed, by the great industrial centres of the north and the banking and commercial authorities in London. During the course of the same day, a number of City financiers warned Asquith against involving Britain in a European conflict and the London Stock Exchange was closed for the first time in its history. Grey threatened to resign if the Morley-Simon declaration was adopted. It did not seem possible that Britain would enter the war under a united Liberal Cabinet.

On the following day, the 1st, Asquith wrote to Venetia Stanley that the Cabinet had come "near to the parting of the ways." Yet on the 2nd, all but two members were converted to a policy of intervention. We now know that one cannot speak of war and anti-war parties; the lines of ministerial difference were too fluid and the views expressed too diverse to make such a neat classification. If there were two small committed groups on either side, there was a far larger group of waverers whose judgments altered with the rapidly changing events. Grey, Asquith (who was particularly concerned with the unity of the party) and Haldane, the old Liberal Imperialist group, were convinced that Britain would have to intervene on the French side. They were joined by the bellicose Churchill. In varying degrees, they were supported by Masterman and Birrell with Crewe, McKenna and Samuel acting as a moderating group. At the other extreme were Burns, Morley, Simon and Beauchamp who opposed any form of involvement. Burns was the most resolute. "Splendid Isolation. No Balance of Power. No incorporation in a continental system" summed up his position. It was one which had nothing in common with Grey's past diplomacy. Not one of these men could lead an anti-war party. Then there was the large group of waverers, reluctant to accept involvement, hopeful of finding a way out of the nightmare, reluctant to face a final decision. Lloyd George, who might have organised an opposition, was not untypical. He was in close touch with Scott of the *Manchester Guardian* and the Liberal opposition. He had not expected war and did not want to fight. Yet he shared Grey's view of the German menace and knew how important the first weeks of war would be. After the 29th, he seemed to waver though there was no clear *casus belli*. Belgium would be for him, as for almost all the others, a way out of an impossible moral dilemma. It would allow him to abandon whatever traditional radical principles he had inherited (and he had already deserted the radical course in foreign matters during the Agadir crisis) without ceasing to claim that heritage.

Events moved rapidly; ministers felt that they were living in a world created by H. G. Wells. But the Cabinet's hesitations arose less from a sense of helplessness than from an understandable unwillingness to face the ultimate question. Confusion and lack of leadership prevented the emergence of an anti-war party; the rapid plunge into actual war, amazingly fast by contemporary standards, made rational thought difficult. Though the German bid for British neutrality was cast aside, the Cabinet continued to avoid final measures. The decision on the 31st, that an expeditionary force should not be sent, convinced some that British participation could be restricted to a naval war. This hope, as Asquith, Grey, Haldane and others knew, invalidated all previous military planning but whatever the deception, it seemed a small price to pay for preserving the unity of the government.

The first major step towards intervention was taken during the long cabinet meeting on Sunday 2 August when Grey raised the question of France's northern coasts. Despite a prolonged discussion lasting almost three hours, and much equivocation on the part of all involved, Grey forced through his demand for a positive answer to the French request. A number of waverers refused to acknowledge any obligation to defend the French but almost all agreed that Britain could not tolerate a hostile power in her home waters. Samuel, attempting to avoid a cabinet division, skillfully combined the two positions. Grey put the Entente case clearly and the crucial decision was taken on his terms. Harcourt, possibly in a moment of panic, appealed to Lloyd George to "speak for us" because it seemed that "Grey wishes to go [to] war without violation of Belgium." Both men accepted the Samuel formula. Grey had secured support for his Entente policy at the expense of only one resignation. John Burns refused to be a party to what he felt to be a step towards war. Morley warned Asquith that in case of war he would also go.

Political considerations contributed to the near unanimity of the Cabinet. It was not that the neutralists deserted their principles to stay in power. Grey's question forced his colleagues to consider those interests which had led them, despite occasional outbursts of indignation, to support an entente policy with its accompanying strategy dispositions right up to the eve of the war. Only a small minority had clearly rejected the balance-of-power theories which underlay Grey's thinking. Few wished to go as far as Grey was now demanding but there was a growing sense that intervention was inevitable. Britain had not been attacked but with France involved, all the past reasons for strengthening the Entente came into play. Politicians seldom resign voluntarily especially for a lost cause. Ministers already knew that if Grey's Entente policy was repudiated, he and Asquith would leave the Cabinet and others would follow. The arrival of the Conservative leaders' letter pledging "to support us in going in with France" strengthened Grey's hand at this crucial meeting. There was a clear alternative to a Liberal government.

The neutralists were uneasy and could not face the full consequences of their choice. This explains the length of the morning Cabinet, the deliberations of the afternoon, the wish to "wait upon events."

The dissenters met. Even before the cabinet meeting, Harcourt, Beauchamp, Pease, Simon and Runciman had joined with Lloyd George to discuss the situation and had come to the hesitant conclusion that none of them was prepared to go to war now. Even this stand was qualified by a reference to "the wholesale invasion of Belgium." After the late-morning cabinet meeting, seven men lunched together at Beauchamp's house which was close to Downing Street. Though there was much talk of following Burns's example, Morley recorded the meeting as "a very shallow affair." The waverers had no wish to break up the government. The "beagles" (Simon, Beauchamp, McKinnon Wood and others) talked and threatened. Morley and Harcourt joined them, as did Lloyd George, who said little. The meeting disbanded without any real decisions reached or action taken. Grey drove to the zoo and spent an hour communing with the birds. Asquith did nothing. At 6 p.m. there was another brief meeting at Lloyd George's home; there had been a further shift in opinion. When the Cabinet met at 6:30, Samuel reported: "the situation was easier, the point of contention was not pressed, and with the exception of the two I have mentioned [Burns and Morley] we remain solid."

It had been known since early morning that German troops had crossed into Luxemburg. The next step could only be an invasion of Belgium. The possibility of such a step was anticipated by most of the Cabinet. The Foreign Office had circulated the French and German reply to its demands for assurances with regard to Belgian neutrality. But those ministers most anxious to keep out of the war did not want to consider the question and neither Asquith nor Grey raised the issue until the invasion became imminent. It was only after most of the waverers had reluctantly concluded that Britain had to intervene that men began to look for a pretext to explain their volte-face. The issue of Belgium was all-important because the radical conscience needed a *raison d'être*. Their followers could not be told that Britain had entered the war to

uphold the balance of power. A German attack on France involved British interests. The Cabinet had resisted this conclusion for many years; ministers now cloaked their final choice in moral terms. The treaty obligation to Belgium provided the necessary justification.

At the evening meeting of the Cabinet on this same packed day, Grey insisted on a strong stand. The majority agreed that a "substantial violation" of Belgian neutrality would compel the government to take action. If the Germans had not gone through Belgium, a larger number of ministers might have resigned. But the majority were already switching to intervention before this final question was considered.

Grey and Asquith had succeeded. The last danger to the unity of the Cabinet arose from the possibility that the Belgians would not resist a German attack. The cabinet decision was reached before Belgian intentions were clear though there were already positive indications. In the very late evening of the 2nd, the news of the German ultimatum to Belgium arrived. On the 3rd, King Albert's appeal for "diplomatic intervention" reached the King and Foreign Office. When the Cabinet met later that morning, ministers concentrated on the details of Grey's speech to the Commons. Nothing further was settled, no decision made to send an ultimatum to Germany, or to declare war, or to send an army to France. Simon and Beauchamp offered their resignations. After Grey addressed the Commons in the afternoon, the Cabinet met again. Asquith convinced the two men to reconsider. The small anti-war group had been routed; apart from Burns only Morley resigned. Their stand had collapsed shattered by the course of events and the determination to enter the war as a united government.

In August 1914 the Cabinet was free to make the ulitmate choice between peace and war. Having put only one foot into Europe in the years which preceded the Sarajevo crisis, it had become necessary to find a reason for taking the ultimate step which would check a German bid for the mastery of Europe. The German invasion of Belgium provided the answer to a dilemma which the Liberals themselves had created. But even in August, they did not wish to pay the full price and until the very end shrank from accepting the bill. A naval war would be an honourable but inexpensive way to safeguard British interests. Grey was not entirely blameless for this last-minute crisis. Like his colleagues, he flinched from abandoning the "free hand" policies of the past. He hoped by his half-committed policies to avoid the final Armageddon and encouraged his colleagues to think along the same lines. He never spelt out the reasons for a continental commitment, or its possible costs. So, at the end of July, he was faced with a hostile Cabinet whose illusions he had encouraged. No one wished to accept the inevitability of British participation in a European war. The result was a long exercise in self-deception. Each illusion that confrontation would not take place was destroyed in turn; the destruction of the last allowed the radicals to appeal to a Gladstonian precedent to explain their acquiescence in the final catastrophe.

Even as the ministers drove to the Commons to hear Grey speak, they knew that the public would support their decision. Holiday crowds, influenced perhaps by their sheer numbers and close proximity to the centre of events, cheered lustily. As was so often the case, it is difficult to know whether Grey's low-keyed address was a genuine reflection of his own inner concern or an intentional effort to exploit those very virtues which had so often swayed the House in his direction. He once more succeeded and his fumbling and hesitant approach, his appeal to the individual conscience of each member, his step-by-step review of Britain's relations to France and finally, almost as a final after-thought, the reference to the question of Belgium, won him the support of the Commons. He argued that Britain's hands were free but showed why members should feel that the French had claims to their support. He suggested that should the German fleet enter the Channel, Belgium, possibly France and probably Holland would lose their independence and British interests

would be engaged quite apart from any treaty obligation. He warned that if Britain ran away she would forfeit all respect and not be in a position at the end of the war to exert her superior strength. Given the careful balance between all the elements which would appeal to his listeners, it is hard not to credit Grey with even greater political acumen than he possessed.

The packed house received Grey's speech well. Bonar Law pledged the Unionist party; Redmond pledged Irish support. When MacDonald spoke in opposition there were murmurs of hostility and some members left the Chamber. Within two days he resigned the leadership of his party to Arthur Henderson. Those radicals and Labour members remaining in opposition were without a voice. In the short adjournment debate which took place in the evening, a number of Liberals denounced the government's policy but Balfour cut the debate short declaring that these men were hardly representative of its members. The Foreign Office was genuinely relieved. Nicolson had waited in "an agony of suspense" before his private secretary assured him that Grey had "a tremendous reception. . .the whole House was with him."

The action was already taking place elsewhere. Even before Grey's speech the Cabinet agreed to warn the Germans against violating Belgian neutrality. The news that German troops had crossed over into Belgian territory reached London at midday. At 2 p.m. Grey, possibly after consultation with Asquith, dispatched a rather mild ultimatum to Berlin asking that the Germans withdraw their demands on Belgium and respect her neutrality. Unless a reply was received in London by 12 p.m. on 4 August, Britain would be obliged to take "all steps in their power necessary to uphold the neutrality of Belgium." When Goschen saw Bethmann at 7 p.m. this request was refused. The ambassador burst into tears and asked for his passports. All of this was an elaborate postscript to the cabinet decisions of 2 July [August, *sic*]. The forms had to be preserved and the actual transition from peace to war conducted in the most formal fashion.

Grey, Asquith, Lloyd George and others waited in the cabinet room for the German reply. It was remembered that midnight in Berlin was 11 p.m. in Britain. The King held a sparsely attended Privy Council meeting at 10:15 and authorised a state of war with Germany from 11 p.m. British time. There was a final muddle. A news agency falsely reported that Germany had declared war on Britain. This had not been anticipated; the note prepared for Prince Lichnowsky was rapidly rewritten and Lancelot Oliphant sent off with it to the German embassy. A few minutes after his return, an *en clair* telegram from Goschen informed the Foreign Office that there would be no German reply to the ultimatum. Young Harold Nicolson was sent to wake Lichnowsky, retrieve the opened incorrect document and substitute the right declaration of war. It was well in keeping with the mores of civilised diplomacy that the ambassador asked Nicolson to give his best regards to his father.

As Big Ben struck eleven, Churchill dispatched his action telegrams to the fleet. The battleships of the First (Grand) fleet were already at Scapa Flow, Cromarty and Rosyth; the Second fleet was in position, the Anglo-French naval plans soon in operation. Naval officers greeted the news of war with relief. On the high seas nothing happened.

L. L. Farrar

THE LIMITS OF CHOICE:
JULY 1914 RECONSIDERED

The study of decision making fascinates historians and political scientists, among others. And some of the most productive, insightful studies on decision making have come since 1960. In these studies the emphasis has often been placed upon how decision makers frame options, make their choice among them, and then move to implement the option selected. This approach has several advantages for the analyst and the student. First, it forces a clearer definition of the choices that actually confronted the harassed decision maker; second, it helps to reveal the precise limits of choice in any given situation; and third, it reminds the scholar that decisions have to be made. Thus if the article by Fritz Stern showed that the responsibility borne by Bethmann Hollweg had limits, the article by L. L. Farrar makes the same point for all the states and leaders involved in the events of July 1914. In this article Farrar, the Oxford-trained historian and author of *The Short War Illusion,* lays out in a precise fashion the basic alternatives before the policymakers in the summer of 1914. And he also seeks to demonstrate how the work of the social scientist can benefit the diplomatic historian. By its very approach and structure this article will enable readers to see for themselves the basic choices present in 1914 and to consider anew the fundamental issues posed by the event of July 1914: Why do wars begin? Why does belligerence sometimes seem more acceptable than peace?

"The Limits of Choice: July 1914 Reconsidered" by L. L. Farrar is reprinted from the *Journal of Conflict Resolution.* Vol. XVI, No. 1 (March, 1972), pp. 1-3, 7-21 by permission of the publisher, Sage Publications, Inc.

THE DISCUSSION of the outbreak of World War I was a classic historical debate. It raised most historical questions. Not only academics but also politicians, journalists, and the educated public became involved. A considerable number of scholars made reputations debating it. It was probably the most burning historical question for the interwar generation and produced a vast quantity of original documents and secondary literature. But the great effort produced little agreement. This paradox seemed to make nonsense of history: the more men knew, the less they agreed. The debate seemed to demonstrate that history is nothing more than national propaganda, subjective prejudice, or intellectual exercise. This conclusion was partially justified since many participants sought immediate political objectives rather than historical objectivity. Indeed it was precisely those political implications of the debate, which attracted public attention, that virtually insured against objectivity. In this sense the debate tells us more about the interwar period than the prewar period. However much the participants genuinely sought to explain the prewar period, their disagreement was due largely to questions of interpretation, since the facts could be generally agreed upon after publication of the official documents. The debate is therefore understandable only if these interpretations are isolated.

The July crisis can be understood in terms of four basic interpretations: responsibility, chance, limited choice, and multiple explanation. The most commonly argued interpretation and starting point for the interwar debate was responsibility. During the war each government had naturally sought to mobilize popular support with the assertion that the enemy was responsible for the war. After the war there was an understandable psychological and political compulsion to believe that someone else had been responsible. The Versailles Treaty established so firmly the concept of responsibility as the framework of debate that at first it was seldom questioned. The concept was applied in varied and frequently contradictory ways. Some argued that all govern-ments to some degree were responsible and that this responsibility could be ranked. Others asserted that only some governments were responsible. Still others blamed specific groups within governments or societies such as the military, revengeful politicians, foreign ministries, conservatives, industrialists, or other interest groups. The concept of responsibility was also interpreted in different ways. Some interpreters perceived conscious decisions to seek war—a responsibility of commission. More found conscious decisions to risk, although not to seek, war—a lessened responsibility of commission. Probably even more saw unconscious willingness to risk war and conscious desire to avoid war—responsibility of omission, that is, statesmen were responsible because they had been irresponsible. Thus responsibility of commission depended primarily on motives, while responsibility of omission depended largely on consequences.

Increasingly the concept of chance competed with responsibility as the interwar years passed. Like responsibility this interpretation had immediate political implications. It seemed to facilitate international reconciliation by justifying the dismantlement of the Versailles Treaty. Its appeal since World War II is the implied warning against precipitating World War III by mistake. It rejected responsibility of commission; since no one had wanted war, no one was responsible. It also rejected responsibility of omission; irresponsibility precluded responsibility. Instead incompetence, weakness, stupidity, miscalculation of risks, and unforeseen events were seen as the real causes of war. Some argued a lack-of-great-man theory: if a great statesman like Bismarck had existed, the war might have been prevented. Many regarded seemingly coincidental events such as the assassination and the military timetables as critical. A few believed a crisis mentality paralyzed statesmen. Still others were even less specific and blamed "fate"—in the sense of bad luck.

The concept of limited choice was specifically advocated by few participants in the debate, but was implied by all those who asserted that the old diplomatic system had caused the war. Like responsibility and chance, limited choice had fundamental political implications. If the international system had caused war to break out in 1914, war might recur unless that system were changed. This interpretation implied rejection of responsibility and chance as explanations for the war following the July crisis. It suggested instead that the cause lay in long-term factors, such as the alliance system, militarism, nationalism, economic competition and imperialism, anachronistic diplomacy, domestic political problems, the press and public opinion, a pervasive sense of doom, and/or "fate"—in the sense of destiny. Some or all of these forces limited so severely the options open to statesmen that war was a virtual certainty once the crisis began.

The concept of multiple explanation became increasingly popular as mounting evidence made the July crisis seem more complex and therefore less susceptible to any single explanation. Like the other interpretations it had fundamental political implications. If the outbreak of war could not be easily explained, it would be difficult to adjust the system in order to avoid its recurrence. Multiple explanation rejected the assumption basic to the other interpretations that *one* cause could be isolated and assumed. Thus all interpretations which perceived *both* long-term (limited choice) *and* short-term (responsibility and chance) causes fall under the general rubric of multiple explanation.

I find limited choice the most satisfactory explanation. Once the crisis began, the choices perceived by European statesmen proved so narrow that war was virtually unavoidable. The fact that other hypothetical choices can be suggested in retrospect does not in itself diminish the usefulness of this interpretation. Instead the critical issue is whether the statesmen of 1914 can realistically be expected to have chosen alternatives which might have avoided war. The perceptions of these statesmen were profoundly affected by the prevailing view of the great-power system and the consequent role of great-power statesmen. All great-power statesmen assumed that it was their primary duty to protect and expand the power of their states by diplomacy if possible, and by war if necessary. When confronted with the choice between a peace which seemed detrimental to their state's interests and a less disadvantageous or even advantageous war, they regarded it as their duty to opt for war. Thus the central problem in understanding the 1914 crisis becomes one of analysing the choices with which the statesmen of 1914 were confronted and of deciding whether or not they could reasonably be expected to have made fundamentally different decisions within the existing conditions. . . .

The interpretation which follows analyzes decisions made during the stages of the crisis. The crisis is herein separated into two general phases, designated as the Austro-Serbian Stage (June 28-July 22) and the European Stage (July 23-August 4). The crisis is divided at July 23—i.e., with the Austro-Hungarian ultimatum to Serbia—because it is seen to mark the point at which generally secret diplomatic preparations end and generally public diplomatic action begins. Clearly the crisis can be divided at other points. For example, Holsti (1970) divided the crisis at July 28 because of increased tension and loss of control. The stages can also be further subdivided. For the present analysis, however, the preparation-action division seems most useful since the behavior during the action phase seems to follow from the decisions made in the preparation stage.

The behavior of statesmen during the crisis is treated in essentially decision-making terms. Within each main stage, the crucial events are identified, the issues implied for each participant are indicated, the hypothetical options suggested, and the actual choices explained. The choices are explained largely in policy terms, i.e., calculations of costs and benefits and of probabilities, rather than in terms of crisis circumstances (stress, anxiety, etc.). These decisions are summarized in Tables 1 and 2 near the beginning of each section discussing one stage of the crisis.

Table 1

Critical Events, Issues, Alternatives, and Choices in the Austro-Serbian Stage of the Crisis (June 28-July 22)

Section	Dates	Government	Event	Issue	Alternatives and choice*
A	June 28-July 5	Austria-Hungary	Assassination of Francis Ferdinand	Austro-Hungarian Policy toward Serbia and self-preservation	(a) Reform of Austria-Hungary (b) Renunciation of Austro-Hungarian great-power status and appeal to other powers (c) *Reprisal against Serbia*
B	July 5	Germany	Austro-Hungarian request for support	Austro-German alliance	(a) Refusal of support to Austria-Hungary (b) Restraint of Austria-Hungary (c) *Reassurance of unqualified support for Austria-Hungary*
C	July 5-22	Germany	Austro-Hungarian response to assassination	Preserve Austria-Hungary and diplomatic victory for Germany and Austria-Hungary	(a) Open involvement (b) *Covert involvement* (c) Noninvolvement
D	July 5-22	Austria-Hungary	Austro-Hungarian response to the assassination	Preparation for military reprisal against Serbia	(a) *Unacceptable ultimatum, then attack* (b) Attack without ultimatum

E	Russia	June 28-July 22	Russian influence in the Balkans	(a) Refuse support to Serbia (b) Reassure Serbia of unqualified support (c) *Restrained support of Serbia*
F	France	June 28-July 22	Franco-Russian alliance	(a) Refuse support to Russia (b) *Reassure Russia of unqualified support* (c) Restrain Russia
G	France	June 28-July 22	Franco-Russian alliance	(a) Refuse support to Serbia (b) Reassure Serbia of unqualified support (c) *Restrained support to Serbia*
H	Britain	June 28-July 22	Status quo, balance of power, and thus peace	(a) Refuse support to France (b) Reassure France of unqualified support (c) Restrain other powers (d) Mediation (e) *Inaction and avoid choice*

*The alternative in italics was the actual choice made.

The Austro-Serbian Stage, June 28-July 22

The assassination of Archduke Francis Ferdinand on June 28, 1914, inaugurated what the Kaiser had presciently predicted would be "the third chapter of the Balkan war in which we shall all become involved. . . ." The assassination forced Austria-Hungary and Serbia into direct confrontation for the first time. The Austro-Serbian crises of the previous eighteen months had proven false beginnings for several reasons. Vienna had not yet become entirely convinced that its existence depended on crushing Serbia. Serbian nationalism had touched the monarchy only indirectly in Albania and in the Balkans in general. The previous crises had remained under the control of the two governments. However, subsequent events culminating in the assassination had altered the situation. Vienna had become increasingly desperate because of the development of the Balkan situation in general. The assassination seemed to prove that Serbian nationalism was a direct—rather than an indirect—threat to the monarchy. It also seemed to demonstrate that relations between the two countries could not be controlled by their governments. In short, the situation had become both more desperate and less containable. . . .

The motives of the assassins and of secret Serbian national societies were probably complex. They may have feared that Austria-Hungary would preserve Albania, establish an anti-Serbian Balkan league, or even resolve the South Slav problem within the monarchy. Conversely they may have been more anxious to activate the moderates in their own government than to anticipate the militants in Vienna. It is equally possible that their thinking was vague but dominated by the anarchist conviction that violence of any kind would serve the cause of Serbian nationalism in some unforeseeable way. The very nature of such secret organizations makes it unlikely that their motives will ever be known precisely. . . .However, their motives are less important than their actions which forced Belgrade and Vienna to confront their irreconcilable objectives.

The ultimate objectives more than the conscious policies of Belgrade and Vienna made a conflict between them virtually unavoidable. Vienna sought unsuccessfully to prove official Serbian complicity. It was unlikely since the assassination faced Belgrade with the awkward choice between making amends or appearing aggressive. It was equally unlikely that the Serbian government could have prevented the assassination since the societies symbolized the national movement and were immensely difficult to control; these considerations made it hard for the Serbian government to move against the societies even after the assassination. The Serbian government therefore contributed in a negative way to the crisis by not preventing the assassination although it did not believe it could have done otherwise. The same may be said of the Austro-Hungarian government. It played a part in the assassination in the sense that Francis Ferdinand presented himself in Sarajevo as a target for assassination. However, the preservation of the monarchy depended in part on its ability to demonstrate Habsburg authority in areas where it was jeopardized by Serbian nationalism. Both Vienna and Belgrade had done what seemed necessary. But what would preserve Austria-Hungary as a great power would provoke Serbian nationalism, and what would satisfy Serbian nationalism would threaten Austria-Hungary as a great power. Thus coexistence seemed virtually impossible and conflict almost inevitable. . . .

The assassination forced Vienna to make a fundamental choice. Hypothetically it had the options of reform, renunciation, and reprisal (see Table 1, Section A). Vienna might have sought to nullify the threat of Serbian nationalism by pacifying the South Slavs inside the monarchy with domestic reform. However, reform was not a practical means of preserving the monarchy since the ruling minorities—particularly the Magyars—probably would have seceded rather than renounce their privileges. Alternatively Vienna might have sought to preserve the existence of the monarchy by renouncing its great-power status and becoming a mandate of the other great powers. This decision was never seriously contemplated since Austria-Hungary—like any state—would consider becoming a mandate only when it had already ceased to be a power and the only alternative was dissolution. Consequently the only option was to remove the threat of Serbian nationalism by reprisal. . . .

This logic seemed to confirm a program which had already been devised in Vienna before the assassination provided the pretext for its implementation. This program reiterated more strongly than ever the Viennese argument for establishing a Balkan league under Austro-Hungarian control and at Serbian expense by the conclusion of an alliance with Bulgaria and the improvement of relations with Romania and Greece. The syndrome of anxiety and arrogance which had become increasingly characteristic of Austro-Hungarian thinking was expressed in the polarization of alternatives: either the monarchy would be preserved by reconstruction and domination of the Balkans or it would collapse. Austro-Hungarian leaders argued for implementation of the program with circular logic. It would succeed if Russia renounced the Balkans. Russia would renounce the Balkans if it were not yet prepared to risk war or if Russian support for Serbia could be made to appear aggressive. The program would fail if Russia refused to renounce the Balkans, but Russian refusal would merely demonstrate that it was already determined to destroy Austria-Hungary. Since Austro-Hungarian chances for survival would diminish with time, an immediate confrontation with Russia was preferable to postponement. Thus either eventuality argued for implementation of the Austro-Hungarian program. . . .

Austro-Hungarian policy is generally criticized but this criticism is misleading. Berchtold is almost universally stigmatized for seeking to preserve a doomed empire at the risk of a European war. Although espoused by pacifists and apologists for the other powers, this criticism could have little relevance for Austro-Hungarian statesmen. It was their duty to preserve Austria-Hungary, not peace. Since they perceived that Austria-Hungary was doomed unless war was

risked, it was their responsibility to risk war. This criticism, directed at Berchtold personally, implies that other Austro-Hungarian statesmen might have acted differently. Although hypothetically possible, it is unlikely; indeed it is more likely that Berchtold postponed rather than precipitated the use of force. Most leading Austro-Hungarian statesmen regarded war with Serbia as necessary even though they recognized that it would probably cause a European war. After initial opposition to the use of force, even Tisza concluded that "we could not do otherwise." Consequently, if Berchtold is criticized, his Austro-Hungarian colleagues must share the responsibility for risking war to preserve their state. However, all great-power statesmen did the same and must therefore share the criticism. In fact, if in contrast to Austria-Hungary the other powers were viable in peace but vulnerable in war, their statesmen must be criticized even more than the statesmen in Vienna. Thus it is inconsistent to criticize Austro-Hungarian policy because it risked war if the European system presupposed that a great power would defend its existence by risking war. In this sense Austro-Hungarian policy was determined by circumstances. . . .

Since Austro-Hungarian domination over Serbia seemed to require Russian renunciation of Serbia which seemed to require German support for Austria-Hungary, Austro-Hungarian domination over Serbia seemed to depend on German support. The Austro-Hungarian request for support confronted German leaders with three hypothetical choices (see Table 1, Section B). They could refuse, restrain, or respond. German policy on the eve of war had shifted among these three courses and could be explained in large measure as an effort to maintain both peace and the alliance with Austria-Hungary, but the Austro-Hungarian request for support necessitated a German choice between maintaining the alliance or the peace. If Germany refused or restrained Vienna in order to preserve peace, it risked Austro-Hungarian dissolution or defection to the Entente and thus the destruction of the alliance. Conversely if it supported Vienna to preserve the alliance, it risked war. In fact, the alliance was jeopardized over the long run even if Berlin supported Vienna's efforts to resolve the dispute with Serbia. The alliance assumed Austro-Hungarian dependence on Germany in the Balkans, particularly with regard to the Austro-Serbian problem. If the Austro-Serbian problem were resolved, as implied by Vienna's request for support, Austria-Hungary would need Germany less and probably pursue a more independent policy. Likewise if Germany no longer supported Austria-Hungary in the Serbian question, Berlin might seek better relations with Russia. Better Russo-German relations would affect the Franco-Russian alliance. Thus the Austro-Serbian dispute was one of the foundation stones not only of the Austro-German alliance but of the whole alliance system. The Germans were therefore faced with an awkward choice between two evils: on the one hand rapid Austro-Hungarian dissolution or defection if they refused or restrained Vienna; on the other, subsequent Austro-Hungarian defection if they supported Vienna. . . .

Berlin's response was determined by its evaluation of the alliance. German great-power status depended in part on Austria-Hungary as a diversion for Russia if war occurred. If war were not perceived as imminent, Germany could refuse or restrain Austria-Hungary in order to preserve peace and seek an alternative to the alliance. Indeed some German diplomats favored the latter course early in the July crisis. If war were perceived as inevitable or even imminent, Germany could not risk the alliance. In the spring of 1914 war seemed increasingly imminent to German leaders, primarily because of Franco-Russian military preparations. At the same time the likelihood of Austro-Hungarian diversion from the Russian front or even dissolution of the monarchy seemed to increase because of problems with Romania and Italy. The assassination seems to have persuaded German leaders not only that an Austro-Serbian *modus vivendi* was impractical but also that the Serbian threat to Austria-Hungary would increase. In short, the prospect of Austro-

Hungarian dependability decreased as the prospect of war increased. Restraining Vienna would only postpone war until a less advantageous juncture when Austria-Hungary was weaker and the Franco-Russian alliance was stronger. Thus German leaders decided that it was necessary to support Vienna. . . .

German support for Vienna implied the eventualities of a German diplomatic victory or immediate war. German leaders hoped several considerations would make a diplomatic victory possible. Russia might not support Serbia, either because Russian military preparations were not completed or because the Tsar might refuse to condone regicide. Even if Russia wanted to support Serbia, France might restrain Russia or at least refuse to support it. Britain might restrain the Franco-Russian alliance or at least refuse to support it. Such eventualities would constitute a German diplomatic victory since they would allow Germany to preserve Austria-Hungary and thus the alliance. They might even shatter the enemy alliance. However, German leaders recognized and assumed the risk of war, for they were aware from the beginning of the crisis that Austria-Hungary planned to attack Serbia, that Russia was unlikely to sacrifice Serbia, that France would probably support Russia, and that Britain might join France. Berlin anticipated this eventuality with circular logic like that used in Vienna. If war did not come in 1914, it was inevitable by 1917. War was preferable in 1914 because Austria-Hungary was stronger and Franco-Russian preparations incomplete. Furthermore, British intervention seemed less certain in 1914 than in 1917 if the Anglo-Russian naval negotiations during the spring of 1914 were an accurate indication of British intentions. Thus either eventuality which could follow from supporting Vienna seemed preferable to the alternative. . . .

German leaders made their decision to support Vienna with even less serious consultation or dissent than their counterparts in Vienna. This has usually been interpreted as proof either of German stupidity or aggressiveness, but it can also be viewed as an indication that German leaders perceived no alternative. Their alternatives had seemed to polarize. On the one hand, restraint of Austria-Hungary seemed to imply its dissolution, thus weakening the Austro-German alliance and constituting a threat to German great-power status; on the other hand, support of Austria-Hungary seemed to imply its revival, thus strengthening of the Austro-German alliance and preserving or even extending German great-power status. Like their Austro-Hungarian counterparts, German leaders were motivated both by anxiety and by arrogance. This mentality insured that they would perceive no alternative compatible with their view of German interests. Indeed, granted their assumptions about German interests and the existing situation, there was none. It would therefore have been both illogical and irresponsible for them to jeopardize German power in order to preserve peace. In this sense, their decision was determined by circumstances.

Having decided to support Vienna the Germans were next confronted with the question of how. Here again they had three hypothetical choices: open involvement, covert involvement, or noninvolvement (see Table 1, Section C). Between its assurance of support to Vienna (on July 5) and the presentation of the Austro-Hungarian ultimatum to Serbia (on July 23), the Germans sought to create conditions conducive to diplomatic or, failing that, military success by supporting Austria-Hungary and confronting Russia with a diplomatic defeat. If Russia were forced to accept diplomatic defeat, the Franco-Russian alliance might be threatened and its ability to conduct war in 1917 jeopardized. Alternatively, if Russia refused to accept diplomatic defeat and opted instead for war, it might improve the chances for German military success in 1914 by alienating Britain and thus forcing the Franco-Russian alliance to fight without British assistance. Consequently far from moderating Austro-Hungarian policy toward Serbia, Berlin urged Vienna to present Europe with a *fait accompli*. By doing so Vienna would not only confront Russia with a diplomatic defeat but would also deter

mediatory proposals which could preclude both Austro-Hungarian revival and an Austro-German diplomatic victory. Meanwhile Berlin pursued these objectives with its own policy of localization which was based on the assertion that the Serbian question was a strictly Austro-Hungarian (i.e., local) rather than European problem. To buttress this assertion and avoid alarming the Franco-Russian Alliance into warning Austria-Hungary or Britain into proposing mediation, Berlin claimed ignorance of Austro-Hungarian intentions and assumed an air of studied calm. However, Berlin also made it clear that the alternative to localization was war, in order to deter Franco-Russian resistance or to make it look like aggression, and thus alienate Britain. Thus Germany opted for covert involvement and pursued the dual policy of encouragement in Vienna but localization elsewhere. . . .

Vienna moved slowly, however. Although Austro-Hungarian leaders were agreed on the aim of a reprisal against Serbia, they were not agreed on the means. They had two basic alternatives: attack with or without diplomatic preparation (see Table 1, Section D). Since other powers—particularly Russia—were unlikely to perceive the assassination as sufficient justification for destroying Serbian independence, Tisza persuaded his colleagues to present Serbia with an ultimatum designed to justify crushing Serbia by making Serbia assume the onus of provocation. This procedure trapped Vienna in a vicious circle, however. Vienna could perhaps justify its destruction of Serbia as far as the other powers were concerned if Serbia rejected an Austro-Hungarian ultimatum, but not if it accepted the ultimatum. Vienna could insure rejection only if it posed unacceptable conditions (which it sought to do). However, Austro-Hungarian reprisal would not seem justified by rejection of unacceptable conditions but only of acceptable conditions. In short, Serbia had to commit suicide to justify its murder by Austria-Hungary. Vienna's ultimatum policy was, however, not only unlikely to succeed but also involved risks for the monarchy. If Serbia accepted the ultimatum, Austria-

Hungary would have to choose between the ultimatum and war. If Vienna abided by the ultimatum, it imposed conditions on itself as much as on Serbia. Conversely if Vienna attacked despite Serbian acceptance, it would appear even more aggressive than if it had attacked Serbia without the ultimatum. Thus although Berlin repeatedly urged haste to insure success, Vienna's delay in formulating the ultimatum probably did not affect its success. In the final analysis Austro-Hungarian policy could not escape its contradictions. . . .

The assassination forced Russian leaders to confront fundamental issues. Like Berlin when asked for support by Vienna, St. Petersburg had the three hypothetical choices of renouncing, reassuring, or restraining Serbia (see Table 1, Section E). Theoretically it was possible that Russia would renounce Serbia, but Russian great-power status assumed the protection of its interests, including its influence in the Balkans which depended in turn on its patronage of Serbia. Thus Serbia depended on Russia which added to the Austro-Serbian tension. Because Russian great-power status depended in part on its support of Serbia, renouncing Serbia was not a viable option. Likewise it was hypothetically possible that Russia could reassure Serbia of its unqualified support, as Berlin had done for Vienna. However, Russian protection of Serbia against Austria-Hungary depended in turn on deterring German support for Austria-Hungary, which was possible by winning French support, and perhaps British support. It was advantageous to avoid alienating Britain by appearing provocative because of unqualified support to Serbia. Consequently unqualified Russian support for Serbia was not practical. Since only restrained support remained, Russia urged Serbia to accept all Austro-Hungarian demands compatible with its independence. This sole recourse in fact served Russian interests by perpetuating Austro-Serbian tension which was a precondition of Russian great-power status. Nonetheless Russian policy was determined by circumstances, in the sense that Russian leaders perceived no viable alternative. . . .

French leaders had the analogous hypothetical choice among the options of refusing, reassuring, or restraining Russia (see Table 1, Section F). It was theoretically possible for them to refuse to support or to restrain Russia, but French great-power status necessitated the alliance with Russia. The alliance assumed Russian dependence on France, which resulted in Russo-German tension and added to Austro-Serbian tension. Consequently a French refusal to support or to restrain Russia was not a valid option. Therefore Paris reassured St. Petersburg of its unqualified support, as Berlin had done for Vienna. Hypothetically France had the same options with Serbia (see Table 1, Section G), but consideration of Britain's reaction precluded such an option—as it did for Russia—and France instead endorsed Russian restraint of Serbia. As in the case of Russia, this sole recourse in fact served French interests by perpetuating Austro-Serbian tension which was a precondition of French great-power status. Nonetheless French policy was determined by circumstances, in the sense that no viable alternative was perceived by French leaders. Thus all the continental powers had committed themselves to policies which had been dictated by events. . . .

Only the British remained uncommitted. Unlike the continental powers, Britain had not yet been forced to make a choice among the options of refusal, reassurance, or restraint (see Table 1, Section H). On the contrary, British interests seemed best served by avoiding this choice as long as possible. British great-power status depended on preserving both its colonial hegemony and the continental balance of power. Both purposes were suited by the existing alliance system. The Austro-German alliance served to perpetuate British colonial hegemony by tying down the Franco-Russian alliance in Europe, and the Franco-Russian alliance helped to preserve the European balance by checking Germany. It was therefore logical that Britain should endeavor to maintain the status quo by preserving peace. However, it was also logical that the continental powers should seek to exploit for their own purposes this British interest in maintaining the status quo. Berlin hoped it could induce London to second the German policy of localization. The British reply, that localization could not succeed if it implied destruction of Serbian independence, was both realistic and also reflected British interests. Localization in the German sense would either resolve the Serbian problem, which was a precondition for the existing alliance system, or precipitate a European war. Meanwhile Paris and St. Petersburg hoped British interest in maintaining the status quo would induce London to restrain Berlin and Vienna. The British refused on the ground that it would thereby jeopardize the possibility of mediation. Instead the British urged a compromise which would preserve the Austro-Serbian problem and avoid the extremes of complete resolution by war, but the compromise-message failed to elicit response. In fact a compromise was impossible since resolution of the Austro-Serbian problem would threaten Russian great-power status and thus the Franco-Russian alliance, and nonresolution would threaten Austro-Hungarian great-power status and thus the Austro-German alliance. Consequently it seemed to London that peace and the status quo might best be preserved by British inaction, since the continental powers might remain cautious as long as Britain remained uncommitted. Thus rather than forcing a British commitment, circumstances forced Britain into noncommitment. However, the logic worked both ways. If Britain could discourage the eruption of an Austro-Serbian crisis by not choosing sides, it could also avoid choosing sides only as long as the crisis did not erupt. A crisis was, however, implicit in the decisions already taken by the continental governments and would become explicit if all abided by these decisions. . . .

The European Stage, July 23-August 4

The first, or Austro-Serbian, stage of the crisis reached its climax and the actual European crisis began with the delivery of the Austro-Hungarian ultimatum to Serbia on July 23. (Measured in terms of published official documents per day of the crisis from June 28 to August 4, the diplomatic activity of the participant governments was between ten and fifteen times as intense after July 23 as before.) The ultimatum implied that Vienna sought a diplomatic victory, under threat of military operations, which would presumably be foregone if the ultimatum were accepted. It confronted the Serbian government with three hypothetical choices: rejection, submission, or humiliation (see Table 2, Section A). Serbia could reject the ultimatum out of hand and thereby risk having to stand alone against Austria-Hungary. Or it could submit completely and thereby renounce its political independence to Austria-Hungary. Or it could win Russo-French support by accepting their advice to navigate between these extremes and to accept a diplomatic humiliation but preserve its independence. Although the Serbian government may have considered the extreme alternatives, it eventually opted for the middle road. In fact, this was the best of all possible choices for Serbia since it would either force Austria-Hungary to recognize Serbia's right to exist if Austria-Hungary accepted, or force Russia to defend Serbia if Austria-Hungary refused. The Entente powers and even the Kaiser reacted with relief to the Serbian reply since it seemed to facilitate the solution least unsatisfactory to the powers—i.e., at Serbian expense but without jeopardizing the balance of power (see Table 2, Section B). Thus as the crisis was about to explode, it seemed most likely to be defused by Serbia's action. . . .

The Serbian answer hypothetically placed Vienna in the awkward situation of choosing between the alternatives of accepting or rejecting (see Table 2, Section C). The Serbs had refused to commit suicide by accepting the ultimatum unqualifiedly or to justify murder by rejecting the ultimatum. Vienna could now accept the Serbian reply and thus win a diplomatic victory at the price of renouncing military operations and recognizing Serbia's right to existence. Or Vienna could reject the Serbian answer and opt instead for military operations at the risk of triggering a European war. A diplo-

Table 2

Critical Events, Issues, Alternatives, and Choices in the European Stage of the Crisis (July 23-August 4)

Section	Dates	Government	Event	Issue	Alternatives and choice*
A	July 23-25	Serbia	Austro-Hungarian ulti-matum	Serbian reply to the ultimatum	(a) Rejection (b) Submission (c) *Humiliation, i.e., qualified acceptance*
B	July 25-26	Russia, France and Britain	Serbian reply to the ultimatum	Conflict between Austria-Hungary and Serbia	(a) Reject Serbian reply (b) *Accept Serbian reply*
C	July 25	Austria-Hungary	Serbian reply to the ultimatum	Conflict with Serbia	(a) Accept Serbian reply (b) *Reject Serbian reply*
D	July 25-31	Germany	Austro-Hungarian rejec-tion of Serbian reply	Austro-German alliance	(a) Restrain Austria-Hungary (b) *Reassure Austria-Hungary of German support*
E	July 25	Russia	Austro-Hungarian rejec-tion of Serbian reply	Russian influence in the Balkans	(a) *Support Serbia* (b) Restrain Serbia (c) Renounce Serbia
F	July 28	Russia	Austro-Hungarian dec-laration of war on Serbia	Russian influence in the Balkans	(a) Submission, or renounce Serbia (b) Continued warnings (c) *Military threat*

	Date	Actor	Situation	Stake	Alternatives
G	July 28-31	Germany	Russian mobilization	Austro-German alliance	(a) Submission (b) *Support Austria-Hungary and military counter-threat against Russia*
H	July 31	Germany	Russian mobilization	French support for Russia	(a) *Military threat against France* (b) No military threat against France
I	July 31	France	German military threat against France	Franco-Russian alliance	(a) Submission (b) *Rejection*
J	July 31	Germany	French rejection of German threat	Austro-German alliance	(a) Revoke threats against France and Russia (b) *Implement threats*
K	July 23-August 4	Britain	Austro-Hungarian ultimatum, Serbian reply, etc.	Status quo, balance of power, and peace	(a) Inaction (b) *Mediation*
L	July 23-August 4	Germany, France, Russia, and Austria-Hungary	British mediation	Austro-German and Franco-Russian alliances	(a) Accept British mediation (b) *Reject British mediation*
M	August 4	Britain	German threat to France (and Belgium)	Franco-British alliance and balance of power	(a) Inaction (b) Renounce France, Belgium, and balance of power (c) *Military counter-threat to Germany*
N	August 4	Germany	British military threat	British entry against Germany	(a) Submission (b) *Rejection*

*The alternative in italics was the actual choice made.

matic victory might have offered the advantages of establishing Austria-Hungary's right to limited intervention into Serbian affairs. It might even have included a European guarantee of Austro-Hungarian existence against Serbia in exchange for an equivalent Austro-Hungarian guarantee to Serbia. However, such a diplomatic victory implied the disadvantage that Europe rather than Austria-Hungary would resolve the Serbian problem. Experience had taught Vienna to expect little satisfaction from the other powers. Above all a compromise solution assumed that Austro-Serbian coexistence was possible, whereas Austro-Hungarian statesmen assumed it was not. In short, the logic of early July still seemed to pertain in late July. Since they were determined to preserve the monarchy, the statesmen in Vienna perceived no choice but to reject the Serbian reply and solve the Serbian problem themselves, even at the risk of European war. . . .

The Austro-Hungarian decision confronted the continental powers with the implications of their policies. The issue was now whether they would abide by their previous decisions at the risk of war or alter their decisions at the risk of their great-power status. Berlin was confronted with the hypothetical choice between restraining or reassuring Vienna (see Table 2, Section D). German leaders may have yielded briefly to the temptation of escaping this choice by finding a compromise solution, but a compromise solution necessitated a fundamental change of German policy which was never seriously considered. On the contrary Berlin encouraged Vienna to begin military operations quickly in order to force a Russian choice between diplomatic defeat and war (see Table 2, Section E). Berlin clarified this choice with its own localization argument that Russian intervention into the Austro-Serbian dispute would constitute aggression against Austria-Hungary. Confronted with this situation the Russians had three hypothetical options: submission, continued diplomatic warnings, or military threat (see Table 2, Section F). They did not seriously consider submission and had become convinced that further diplomatic warnings were

pointless. They therefore sought to restructure the issue from the German contention of localization to Europeanization with the assertion that the Austro-Serbian problem was European, not strictly Austro-Hungarian. This formula would constitute diplomatic victory for Russia and diplomatic defeat for Austria-Hungary since it would institutionalize Serbian independence and thus Austro-Hungarian insecurity. Meanwhile Russia rejected a diplomatic defeat as implied in the Austro-Hungarian declaration of war on Serbia. Russian leaders demonstrated that they preferred war to diplomatic defeat by announcing mobilization first against Austria-Hungary and then against Germany. In short they presented Germany with the choice between diplomatic defeat and war. The Germans rejected the Russian threats and replied with their own threat of mobilization (see Table 2, Section G), but the German counter-threat was rejected in turn by the Russians. Thus threats of war had failed to make Serbia, Austria-Hungary, Russia, or Germany accept diplomatic defeat. . . .

Diplomatic defeat might have been accepted only if a threat of war had been credible, but none could have been credible. Such a threat can be credible only if it implies immediate defeat. Immediate defeat assumes concentration of forces, but none of these powers concentrated against any of the others, because doing so would have contradicted basic strategic and diplomatic assumptions. Austria-Hungary did not concentrate its forces against Serbia because it assumed that it would be unnecessary if Russia renounced Serbia and impossible if Russia supported Serbia. Russia did not concentrate its forces against Austria-Hungary or Germany because it assumed that it would be necessary to fight both or neither. If it fought both, it preferred to divide its forces. Germany did not concentrate against Russia because it too assumed that it would have to fight both France and Russia or neither. If it fought both, it preferred to concentrate on France. Thus none of these threats succeeded because none was coordinated with basic strategic and diplomatic assumptions.

They might have succeeded had these assumptions proven fallacious, but the threats were necessary only if the assumptions were valid. Thus the threats of war could have succeeded only if they had been unnecessary and failed when they were necessary. However, the threats had to succeed if war were to be avoided, and so war could not be avoided by Austro-Hungarian, Russian, or German threats against one another.

War might have been avoided, however, if France accepted diplomatic defeat, which it might have done had a German threat been credible—if it were threatened with immediate military defeat by Germany's concentrating forces against it. In fact, German strategists did plan a concentration against France precisely because they believed it could be defeated quickly (whereas Russia could not) and because doing so corresponded with their basic strategic and diplomatic assumptions. German leaders assumed Germany would have to fight both Russia and France or neither, because Russia would opt for war only if supported by France. Thus French decisions rather than German threats would determine Russian policy. French decisions could be affected only by a German threat to France. It was therefore appropriate that this was the only threat German strategists prepared. It was also the only threat during the crisis which coordinated military strategy with diplomatic policy in the sense of confronting France with the possibility of immediate defeat (see Table 2, Section H). Like the previous threats it did not necessitate war, since it offered the French the alternative of diplomatic defeat. The French were consequently confronted with the choice between diplomatic defeat and war (see Table 2, Section I). The French rejection implied that the German threat was not credible. Perhaps no threat would have been credible if diplomatic defeat was not conceivable because a defeat required renouncing Russia and thus French great-power status. The French refusal confronted Germany with a hypothetical choice between diplomatic defeat and war (see Table 2, Section J). Berlin might have chosen diplomatic defeat if it had felt

that the war could not be won or that the price of winning would be too high, i.e., if the long-run Franco-Russian threat had been credible. However, diplomatic defeat implied renunciation of Austria-Hungary and thus German great-power status. The Germans therefore opted for war instead of diplomatic defeat. The French and German decisions demonstrated that no military threat was sufficiently credible to make the continental powers accept a diplomatic defeat which implied loss of great-power status. War was avoidable only if diplomatic defeat was acceptable because the threat of war was credible. Thus war was unavoidable. . . .

The only escape from this logic seemed to be British mediation. The Austro-Hungarian ultimatum to Serbia confronted Britain with the hypothetical alternatives of inaction or mediation (see Table 2, Section K). Since inaction implied genuine disinterest, it was not acceptable to the British. Mediation was therefore undertaken because it implied preservation of the status quo and thus Britain's pivotal position in the balance of power. Britain confronted the continental powers with the choice of accepting or rejecting mediation (see Table 2, Section L). British mediation could succeed only as long as the balance of power was accepted by all the powers. The powers would do so as long as they believed it was unnecessary to change it in order to preserve their great-power status. British mediation might therefore have succeeded before the assassination, but then it had seemed unnecessary and undesirable to the British. It seemed necessary only after the assassination, in fact only after the ultimatum. However, the ultimatum indicated that the balance of power was no longer accepted by all the continental governments. Austria-Hungary and Germany had committed themselves to alter it by destroying Serbian independence in order to preserve their own great-power status. France and Russia had committed themselves to defend Serbian independence in order to preserve their great-power status. These two positions were irreconcilable and British mediation could have succeeded only if one side had been willing to accept diplomatic defeat. None would do so since each equated diplomatic defeat with loss of great-power status, and British mediation could therefore not have succeeded after the ultimatum, or even the assassination. Thus it was caught in a paradox; it could succeed when it seemed unnecessary and could not succeed when it did seem necessary. The fact that mediation was tried is frequently interpreted as proof that it was practical but it failed because of British mistakes. This criticism is unjustifiable and misleading. British mediatory efforts were not a case of losing peace by mistake but of mistaken efforts to save peace when it was already lost. . . .

The only remaining possibility for preserving peace seemed to be a threat of British intervention against Germany. The rejection of their mediatory efforts forced the British to choose among the options of inaction, renunciation of the alliance with France, and intervention against Germany (see Table 2, Section M). Both inaction and renunciation of the alliance with France seemed to imply French defeat, the end of French great-power status, and thus disruption of the balance of power. Since Britain regarded these eventualities as unacceptable, no choice existed but the threat of intervention against Germany. Such a threat could succeed only if it kept Germany from committing itself to change the balance of power. Germany might not do so if it believed British intervention could preclude victory. A threat of British intervention might therefore have succeeded before the assassination, but before the assassination it seemed unnecessary. It seemed necessary only after mediation had failed, but the failure of mediation indicated that Germany had committed itself to change the balance of power. The threat of British intervention could then have succeeded only if Germany had been willing to accept diplomatic defeat. Germany would have accepted diplomatic defeat if it believed British intervention would preclude victory. Although German leaders believed British intervention would reduce their chances (and therefore sought to keep Britain neutral), they did not expect

it to preclude victory. The British threat thereby proved no more credible than the other threats. Perhaps none could have proven credible since German leaders equated diplomatic defeat with renunciation of great-power status. In short, British intervention could not succeed after mediation had failed or even after the assassination. Thus it again was caught in a paradox like mediation. It could succeed when it seemed unnecessary and could not succeed when it did seem necessary. The fact that it was tested is frequently interpreted as proof that it was practical but that it failed because of British mistakes. Again, as with mediation, this criticism is unjustifiable and misleading; the British threat of intervention was not a case of losing peace by mistake but of a mistaken effort to save peace when it was already lost. . . .

Conclusions: The Limits of Choice

Each power did what seemed necessary to remain a power. All perceived a choice among diplomatic victory, diplomatic defeat, and war. All preferred diplomatic victory since it implied the rewards of war without the risks, but one power could win diplomatic victory only if another accepted diplomatic defeat. All rejected diplomatic defeat since it implied the price of military defeat without the possibility of victory. War at least implied the possibility of victory as well as defeat. Thus diplomatic victory was impossible because diplomatic defeat was inconceivable, whereas war was conceivable. Consequently when a choice seemed imperative, war became inevitable.

The interpretation suggested here has implications for our understanding of the 1914 crisis. Traditionally most historical studies of the crisis have presented it as the result of design, blunder, chance, or some combination. More recently social scientists have argued that it was the result of circumstantial factors (e.g., stress, hostility, etc.). Few studies have perceived the crisis as the logical result of rational policy considerations. This article has sought to fill this gap. Only by having all possible views of the crisis can we fully understand its complexity.

CONCLUSION

HISTORICAL study illuminates, clarifies, and makes precise our knowledge of the past. Often historians repeatedly study the same issue or problem, attacking it from different angles, with different assumptions, and with different results. But historical writing is not circular, or at least, should not be so. It is cumulative. Historians do learn from each other, even those of widely different views. Some facts and generalizations do become accepted as valid. This is as true for the origins of World War I as for other watershed events. The conclusions that follow do not explain why war came in the summer of 1914; rather they are a start in explaining why it came. They remain a base point to which other interpretations and views can be added and from which other research may flow.

A series of broad observations must come first. Of these the linkage between long-term and short-term causes is the most important. The outbreak of the war cannot properly be understood in a vacuum. The war did not suddenly erupt. Its roots lay well back into the past. Among these linkages the existence of alliance and entente systems was the most important. Not only did they permanently divide Europe into different political camps; they created expectations of support and group loyalty that influenced the way statesmen assessed their country's options and obligations. And so it happened in 1914.

The imperial frictions of the early twentieth century exacerbated alliance relationships and brought Great Britain into the system through its ententes with France and Russia. Yet while overseas imperialism sharpened the divisions between the powers, it had less impact upon European diplomacy after 1911. Instead, from 1912 to July 1914 Balkan issues dominated the agenda. As Turkish power receded, the imperial knives were sharpened—in anticipation of a meal that the European powers had long dreaded. And it was just this familiarity and intensity that made a Balkan issue so much more dangerous than an overseas, colonial clash such as over Morocco.

The alliance and entente system had other consequences as well. One was the reinforcement it gave to the rampant militarism and navalism that characterized the years before 1914. Arms races, expanding armies, aborted naval negotiations, and the incessant fear of "falling behind" eroded any stable conception of security. Propaganda campaigns and a bellicose military and naval press also inflamed the situation. Moreover, as warfare became a seemingly more "professional" enterprise, the alleged ability of civilians to understand it (or to be entitled to control it) diminished. No longer could statesmen deliberate calmly and for lengthy periods; now the premium was on decisiveness, surprise, and execution. In 1914 glib assurances and intricate war plans based upon a "best case analysis" propelled many decisions. From General Conrad in Vienna to his counterparts elsewhere it was the military leaders who determined the timing. In the world of political-military decision making, the military prevailed.

A generation ago historians stressed the role of the popular press and economics upon the coming of the war. Now they do so less confidently. Public opinion and its impact upon decision makers are treated skeptically. The press played a role but certainly not a decisive one in the events of July 1914. Nor are the economic explanations for the war so convincing. To be sure different countries had significant economic problems, even severe ones, but none went to war to cure its economic ills. The war was not, despite what Lenin believed, the last stage of finance capitalism. If anything, the financiers were the most passive and hesitant of all the elites. Economics formed a key framework for the decision makers, but their world remained (dangerously so) the world of aristocratic statesmen, often ill-informed royalty, and a military and naval elite.

A final, long-term consideration deserves mention: the role of nationalism. A Bosnian nationalist fired the shots at Sarajevo. His act set in motion the decisions that would bring the war, and the end of that war would see triumphant nationalism enshrined. The tide loosed by the French revolution would have a still further set of impacts as new states appeared. Yet the war suggested a need to overcome nationalism with an international league of nations. Paradoxically nationalism, which was a cause of the war, would be ratified by the war and made still more difficult to overcome.

It is now time to shift from general conclusions to specific, country by country, observations. In each case the treatment is brief. The reader is expected to fill in the blanks and to add further details.

Germany: In 1914 the Second Reich verged dangerously close to internal upheaval. Significant domestic problems—economic, constitutional, political—put the ruling groups on the defensive and on edge. A reckless naval policy exacerbated relations with Britain; a military approach to political and diplomatic issues meanwhile threatened to escalate the importance of any event. Nevertheless, Germany did not plot the war in 1914. Rather, in the July crisis it was not—as it had been even a year before—a force for restraint and caution. A more cautious Germany might have prevented the war; the Germany of Kaiser Wilhelm II and Bethmann Hollweg did precisely the opposite. They took risks, gave Vienna a "blank check," miscalculated, and almost fatalistically allowed events to dominate. The result was a world war.

Russia: Domestic pressures also existed in Russia, but these are less important to an understanding of tsarist foreign policy than is true for Germany. Rather Pan-Slavism, a fixation on the Straits question, and a certain recklessness toward the Balkans and the Habsburg monarchy are more important. Prestige, a fear of exclusion from the lower Balkans, and a sense of commitment to Serbia prompted the decisions of 1914. Regrettably, possibly no government or civilian leadership less understood the complexities of mobilization and military decision making than that in St. Petersburg. Thus its actions of July 25 (measures preliminary to mobilization) and of July 30 (general mobilization) accelerated a dangerous situation, possibly without a full recognition of the risks.

Austria-Hungary: The Danubian government wanted first of all to maintain the status quo. The Habsburgs not only faced the mounting Slav challenge and troubles with the Magyars, but the prospect of the death of the octogenarian emperor and an uncertain constitutional future. The loss of prestige and of both relative and absolute power in the Balkans after the autumn of 1912 reinforced a pervasive sense of frustration. Three times in 1912 and 1913 the monarchy nearly went to war with Serbia. After Sarajevo, Vienna resolved upon a local war to punish Serbia without worrying about whether it would expand into a world war. In the 1914 crisis Austria-Hungary would be the great protagonist. It would be the state that determined the timing of the crisis. With this in mind the details of its actions are rather less important. The leadership of the monarchy wanted war, might have fought even had Berlin said no, and in the end got the war they hoped would break the South Slav menace. Instead it broke the monarchy.

Britain: Since 1900 London had drawn closer to continental affairs without becoming totally entangled. It sought to play the informal balancer; in actuality it always sided with the Franco-Russian camp. In 1914 the Irish crisis helped to mask the seriousness of the Balkan situation. Yet Grey's diplomacy was curiously ineffective for such an experienced foreign minister. His efforts to mediate in late July now seem less important and more halfhearted than earlier historians thought, his irresponsibility greater. London had its own measure of fatalism as well.

Serbia: Belgrade played the most reckless role, allowing its internal political squabbles to culminate in the murders at Sarajevo. Yet the frustrations experienced by Belgrade in dealing with the Habsburgs and the heady wine of the military victories of 1912-1913 made self-restraint difficult. Once Vienna resolved for war, Serbia had no option but to plot how best to defend itself, at home and abroad. And in this Russian support was imperative. Once it came, Serbia had a chance; but the chances of preventing a European war were also at an end.

France: Successive French governments came to see in Russia the only protection against Germany. Yet none had really anticipated the situation when support of Russia might bring the very German attack that the French so feared. In 1914 the French leadership gave the tsarist government too much unqualified support too early. As a result, Paris lost the crucial leverage that might have convinced St. Petersburg to be less impetuous. In any event, the French were in a weak position and made it weaker.

Italy: Rome had no role in the outbreak of the war in 1914. But its attack on Tripoli in 1911 marked the first salvo against Turkey. This in turn encouraged both Russia and the Balkan states to create the Balkan League and then, in October 1912, to attack Turkey. From that point, the chances of a war involving Austria-Hungary multiplied greatly, and so did those of a possible European war.

There are many possible lessons to be learned from the origins of World War I. But historians hesitate to state them dogmatically. One, however, must be asserted unequivocally: a war came in the summer of 1914 and it could happen again. The recent public success of General Hackett's fictional account, *The Third World War: August 1985,* is a sober reminder that 1914 could have an echo later. Neither the public nor its civilian leaders can afford to ignore some of the basic mistakes of 1914; above all, leaders need to be deliberate, to keep options open, to communicate, to keep the military in check, and to contemplate the question of what happens if military plans go astray. Civilization would be far better served if the last line of T. S. Eliot's "The Hollow Men" remained its epitaph: "This is the way the world ends, not with a bang but a whimper."

SUGGESTIONS FOR ADDITIONAL READING

THE VOLUME of historical literature and memoirs on the origins of World War I is nearly overwhelming. The suggestions that follow provide an introduction for the student and point the way to still other studies.

For the student who wishes to go beyond a textbook account of the coming of the war, four short works offer more detail: Laurence Lafore, *The Long Fuse* (2nd ed., New York, 1971); Joachim Remak, *The Origins of World War I, 1871-1914* (New York, 1976); L. F. C. Fuller, *Origins of the First World War* (New York, 1970); and Jacques Droz, *Les causes de la première guerre mondiale: Essai d'historiographie* (Paris, 1973). For a slightly longer study, with documents, see Imanuel Geiss, *July 1914: The Outbreak of the First World War* (New York, 1967). A very readable, if somewhat misleading, account is Barbara Tuchman, *The Guns of August* (New York, 1961).

For more exhaustive examinations of the war in its broader context, see S. B. Fay, *The Origins of the World War* (2nd. ed., 2 vols. in one; New York, 1930) which argues the moderate revisionist position. Pierre Renouvin, *La crise européenne et la première guerre mondiale, 1904-1918* (5th ed., Paris, 1969); Bernadotte Schmitt, *The Coming of the War, 1914* (2 vols., New York, 1930); and Luigi Albertini, *The Origins of the War of 1914* (3 vols., London, 1952-1957) take an anti-German posture.

On the conspiracy to assassinate the Archduke Franz Ferdinand, Vladimir Dedijer, *The Road to Sarajevo* (New York, 1966) is sympathetic and insightful. Three more recent and general works are O. J. Hale, *The Great Illusion, 1900-1914* (New York, 1971); Dwight E. Lee, *Europe's Crucial Years: The Diplomatic Background of World War I, 1902-1914* (Hanover, N.H., 1974); and Erwin Hölzle, *Die Selbstentmachtung Europas: Das Experiment des Friedens vor und im Ersten Weltkrieg* (Göttingen, 1975).

For the longer-term background of the war, the two massive and still splendid studies by William L. Langer remain indispensable: *European Alliances and Alignments, 1870-1890* (New York, 1933) and *The Diplomacy of Imperialism* (2nd. ed., 2 vols. in one; New York, 1951). Also see the provocative if occasionally exasperating study by A. J. P. Taylor, *The Struggle for Mastery in Europe, 1848-1918* (Oxford, 1954).

There are numerous collections of articles on the July crisis and on the differences of historical opinion about it. Among these the following are especially helpful: Dwight Lee (ed.), *The Outbreak of the First World War: Causes and Responsibilities* (Lexington, Mass., 1975); H. W. Koch (ed.), *The Origins of the First World War: Great Power Rivalry and War Aims* (New York, 1972); Joachim Remak (ed.), *The First World War, Causes, Conduct, Consequences* (New York, 1971); Walter Laqueur and George L. Mosse (eds.), *The Coming of the First World War* (New York, 1966).

Many of the most useful studies focus on the role of a single country or pair of countries in the years before 1914. For Austria-Hungary see F. R. Bridge, *From Sadowa to Sarajevo* (London, 1972) and *Great Britain and Austria-Hungary, 1906-1914* (London, 1972); Norman Stone, *The Eastern Front, 1914-1917* (London, 1967); Paul Schroeder, "World War I as Galloping Gertie: A Reply to Joachim Remak," *Journal of Modern History,* Vol. XLIV (1972), pp. 319-345; and two articles by the editor of these readings, "Influence, Power, and the Policy Process: The Case of Franz Ferdinand, 1906-1914," *The Historical Journal,* Vol. XVII (1974), pp. 417-434, and "Theories of Organizational Process and Foreign Policy Outcomes," in *Diplomacy: New Approaches in History, Theory, and Policy,* ed. Paul Gordon Lauren (New York, 1979), pp. 137-161. The older study by E. C. Helmreich, *The Diplomacy of the Balkan*

Wars, 1912-1913 (Cambridge, Mass., 1938) remains valuable.

For Britain see Zara Steiner, *Britain and the Origins of the First World War* (New York, 1977) and its very useful bibliography; also F. H. Hinsley (ed.), *The Foreign Policy of Sir Edward Grey* (Cambridge, Eng., 1977); and K. G. Robbins, *Sir Edward Grey* (London, 1971).

For France there are far fewer monographs; one that helps is Christopher Andrew's *Théophile Delcassé and the Making of the Entente Cordiale, 1898-1905* (London, 1968). Also Keith Eubank, *Paul Cambon: Master Diplomatist* (Norman, Okla., 1960), and the older work by E. Malcolm Carroll, *French Public Opinion and Foreign Affairs, 1871-1914* (New York, 1931) remain quite useful.

On Germany the detailed works are numerous. See Fischer's two major works, *Germany's Aims in the First World War* (New York, 1967) and *The War of Illusions* (New York, 1975); Volker Berghahn, *Germany and the Approach of War in 1914* (London, 1973); Imanuel Geiss, *German Foreign Policy* (London, 1976); Hermann Kantorowicz, *Gutachten zur Kriegschuldfrage 1914*, ed. Imanuel Geiss (Frankfurt a.M., 1967). On the Fischer controversy see John Moses' analysis, *The Politics of Illusion: The Fischer Controversy in German Historiography* (London, 1975), and Konrad Jarausch, *The Enigmatic Chancellor: Bethmann Hollweg and the Hybris of Imperial Germany* (Princeton, 1972). For the work of a major East German historian see Fritz Klein's *Studien zum deutschen Imperialismus vor 1914* (Berlin, 1976).

For Italy and Russia the student must remain content with standard textbook accounts.

In the last decade a series of specialized books have appeared on aspects of the process that led to war. On the foreign offices, see Zara Steiner, *The Foreign Office and British Foreign Policy, 1898-1914* (Cambridge, Eng., 1969); Lamar Cecil, *The German Diplomatic Service, 1871-1914* (Princeton, 1976); Paul G. Lauren, *Diplomats and Bureaucrats* (Stanford, 1976).

On military and defense planning, see Paul Halpern, *The Mediterranean Naval Situation, 1908-1914* (Cambridge, Mass., 1971); Nicholas d'Ombrain, *War Machinery and High Policy* (Oxford, 1973); John Gooch, *The Plans of War: The General Staff and British Military Strategy, 1907-1916* (Oxford, 1974); Gunther Rothenberg, *The Army of Francis Joseph* (East Lafayette, Ind., 1976); Gerhard Ritter, *The Sword and Sceptre* (4 vols., Miami, 1969-1973); and the editor's *The Politics of Grand Strategy: Britain and France Prepare for War, 1904-1914* (Cambridge, Mass., 1969). The war plans of the various powers are collected in Paul Kennedy (ed.), *The War Plans of the Great Powers* (London, 1979).

On economic policies, René Poidevin, *Les relations économiques et financières entre la France et l'Allemagne de 1898 à 1914* (Paris, 1969) is particularly useful; the older study by Herbert Feis, *Europe: The World's Banker, 1870-1914* (New Haven, 1930) remains valuable, as does Rondo E. Cameron, *France and the Economic Development of Europe, 1800-1914* (Princeton, 1960).

Since 1960 a number of political scientists have written about the origins of World War I, using it as a case study in their attempts to quantify the study of international relations. Of those studies three deserve attention if not total respect: Nazli Choucri and Robert C. North, *Nations in Conflict: Domestic Growth and International Violence* (San Francisco, 1975); Ole R. Holsti, *Crisis Escalation War* (Montreal, 1971); Eugenia V. Nomikos and Robert C. North, *International Crisis: The Outbreak of World War I* (Montreal, 1976).

For the student who wishes to study the diplomatic documents on both the background and the actual 1914 crisis, Geiss' volume, already noted, is an excellent beginning. Also see his massive collection of documents (in German), *Julikrise und Kriegsausbruch 1914* (2 vols., Hanover, 1934-1964). Any of the studies cited will give further bibliographical information on the major document collections.

The memoir literature is vast, but students will find a sampling of it rewarding, especially the volumes by Grey and Bethmann Hollweg (both for what they say and what they carefully do not say). Nor can one fail to note Winston Churchill's monumental account, part memoir, part history, and part patriotic manifesto, *The World Crisis, 1911-1918* (New York, 1923-1929); it remains a must.